IT'S TIME

What You Don't Know Can Hurt You

Eye Openers In Ephesians!
Real Life Identity
From A
Coach's Perspective

AUTHOR:

Carolyn Freeman

"Perhaps the grandest of all Paul's Epistles. Ephesians is needed more today than ever. Carolyn Freeman will elucidate the blessings we enjoy, the behavior needed, and even warn of the battle we face in our society each and every day. Practical always, funny at times, yet entirely serious in her approach to our Beloved in this book."

Dr. Terry Faulkenbury
Senior Pastor of West Cabarrus Church
Associate Professor of Liberty University Rawlings School of Divinityt's

It's Time is a book whose time has definitely come! Most people have no idea that Jesus has "raised us to sit together in heavenly places" with Him. It is a life-changing truth to say the least. The most powerful thing about this book is that the author actually lives experientially in that place, so she is able to write and speak in such a way that others can understand that place is for them too.

Terri Broome, Director of Women's Ministry at Pursuit Church and author of *The Ordinary Road.*

"Carolyn's gift of Coaching and mentoring women comes from a place far beyond her credentials. It comes from her own real life journey of experiencing God's grace and learning to live it out daily. God is using Carolyn to coach and teach others what it means to actually LIVE in grace and walk in the TRUE freedom that we all long for. The words of these pages are filled with authentic, honest, and deeply encouraging"but God" moments. I highly recommend!"

Sheila Treat CPLC
Vice President of ReJoy Ministries

"This is a delightful 'must read' written from a coaching perspective in a conversation style. Carolyn writes with guidance and encouragement for ladies of all ages. Her life coaching skills and deep experience in teaching God's word is evident in her writing. As you unpack this study, you will learn from one of the best.

Becky Seamon
National Walk Thru The Bible Instructor
Women's Director of West Cabarrus Church

"Vulnerable and at times witty, Carolyn Freeman's book, It's Time: What You Don't Know Can Hurt You, is written in a style that positions you across the table from her with a hot cup of coffee in hand. Her dive into the Book of Ephesians will leave you encouraged and with practical suggestions and life-changing truth. Her love for others is evident in every story she tells. Her love for God shines out from the pages, beckoning you to join her and discover the true freedom only found in Christ."

Cortney Donelson
Author of Clay Pot Cracked
Speaker & Marriage Mentor
Director Of Operations, icuTalks

"My daughter walked away from the Lord and into an emotionally and spiritually abusive relationship. Five years later, on an autumn afternoon, we received a call that her heart had been broken to pieces. As my husband and I drove to be with her,
I knew the first call I needed to make was to ReJoy Ministries. We had astonishing privilege to watch our daughter come back to new life and be restored with a vivaciousness that can only be described as a miracle! I credit Carolyn for the full restoration in Jesus that our sweet girl now has. In this book, Carolyn shares through the backdrop of Ephesians, how what you don't know CAN hurt you and be assured it can and will. You DON'T want to miss this amazing piece of work by this remarkable Christian Life Coach, Carolyn Freeman."

Shari Braendel
Founder of Faith Meets Fashion
Author of Help Me, Jesus, I Have Nothing To Wear

Dedicated to
Hannah Elizabeth Freeman
Our precious granddaughter
Entered life September 19, 2008
Entered Life Eternal
September 24, 2008
"Gone but not forgotten"

Love you Hannah

Contents

Foreword

Cherished one, life isn't easy. Often it does not turn out as we expected or   planned when we charted our life course. We have all had broken dreams, relational disappointments, and choices that maybe weren't wise in the moment. What do you do when there seems to be nothing you can do? Where do you go? Who can you trust to talk to about important situations? Good questions. I often   asked myself those same questions while amid life's many ups and downs.

My story is probably similar to many of your stories. I married young and started a family, procuring lofty dreams and high hopes for my children. Ten years into the marriage and four children later, things began to fall apart. All four children had medical issues that brought heavy financial problems. The toll on our marriage and family became one crisis intervention after another. Struggles with depression and anxiety became the "norm" around our house. Alcohol and drug addiction in our immediate and extended family threw a monkey wrench into the whole family relational dynamics. I found myself in many difficult situations where I needed a confidante, someone who would just come alongside me and walk with me through this painful journey.

I was blessed to have a few individuals that the Lord handpicked to be in my life at just the right time to walk me to the right Person. These chosen ones made all the difference in the world during these critical, life-changing events. Had these people not walked with me on my journey in a non-judgmental and grace-filled way, I do not believe I would be here today. I am amazed and awed that the Sovereign Lord of love and light saw me as the apple of His eye, as He has you. This intimate knowledge can either prompt us to run and hide or it will call us to come out of our pain into healing. Come and meet our Jehovah Rapha, the God who heals face to face!

If you are living in the deep depths of chaos, crisis, addiction, anxiety, depression, or grief, it would be my great joy to join you on your journey. Brokenness had been a constant companion for much of my adult life, but the Lord had surprising ways to break into my brokenness. He wants to break into yours as well. His purpose is not just your healing but to show you who you were created to be before the pain and suffering set up house in your heart. He has an astounding story to retell in His redemptive mercy and grace He is calling you to experience. The invitation is deep, and the door is open wide as He is calling you into His presence now. We are never too broken or hopeless that He cannot do another one of His marvelous miracles. It's time here and now. Join me as we journey together through Ephesians to learn things we might not know that will make all the difference for time and for eternity.

x

Acknowledgments

My deepest thanks goes to the many hands that have joined me during the journey of getting this truth out on these pages. At the top of the list is Peggy Kean who has been my sounding board, confidante, and proofreader. She is a fellow writer and has been a lifesaver. Lisa Haimbaugh has been my enthusiastic cheerleader, offering to type the final manuscript. She was a strong support when I needed it most. Becky Seamon, my dear friend, knows the inside story of creative writing. The prayers and words she spoke over me kept me on course as I faced the challenge of revision after revision, one word at a time. Thank you, Heather McGinnis for proofreading the manuscript. To my friend and fellow author Cortney Donelson, thank you for editing the manuscript and finalizing it before publication.

My two sisters, Sandy Ladd and Jan Batts, are always there for me. I am thankful that our lives as little girls on a farm gave us plenty of stories to tell. I am still trying to retell the story they've told about me all these years. We laugh about how we all see it from different perspectives. We live and die together. We are learning to laugh and to cherish each other more as we grow older and continue to make memories. The love we have for each other is an unbreakable bond even when we don't agree. Just call us the golden girls as we are older, but funnier in my opinion and that is my story! I am telling the story now, girls.

To my daughter, Christy Freeman, I owe a debt of love for many reasons. She assisted me with Chapter 6 with her creative artwork and by believing in her Mom. She is one of the best graphic artists I know. She lived through the story. Healing is so precious when you see it happen in the next generation. Momma loves you, Christy, to the moon and back.

To my young friend, Trevor King, who has a heart that pants after God and a creative artistic hand as well. Thank you for "the armor." Trevor, you have great potential. Use it.

Thanks to my fashionable friend, Shari Braendel, who trusted her most precious gift to me as we coached her daughter back to Jesus. Shari has placed many of her precious girls from her small group in our hands at ReJoy

Ministries to find healing and wholeness. Thank you for caring for your girls with such love.

To my two partners at ReJoy Ministries, Patti Hedge and Sheila Treat, we walk together as one. We walk with our clients to freedom as they find out "who they really are in Christ." I love you both dearly.

My final thanks goes out to my family. My husband, my four grown children, and my ten grandchildren: Catherine, Josiah, Victoria, Hannah (in Heaven), Zachary, Abigail, Aaron, Justin, Harrison, and Madeline. They love Maw Maw, "warts and all." I love my grandchildren with a passion. This is our next generation; we are passing on the baton as they follow hard after Christ. My greatest desire and deepest prayer is that they will fall deeply in love with Jesus Christ the "Lover of their souls." When they do they will experience the deepest joy and greatest satisfaction to which nothing in this world can compare. For me to live is Christ, my highest honor I can give the One who gave His all for me. I love you, Lord. It is "Yes, Lord" all the way to the Pearly Gates.

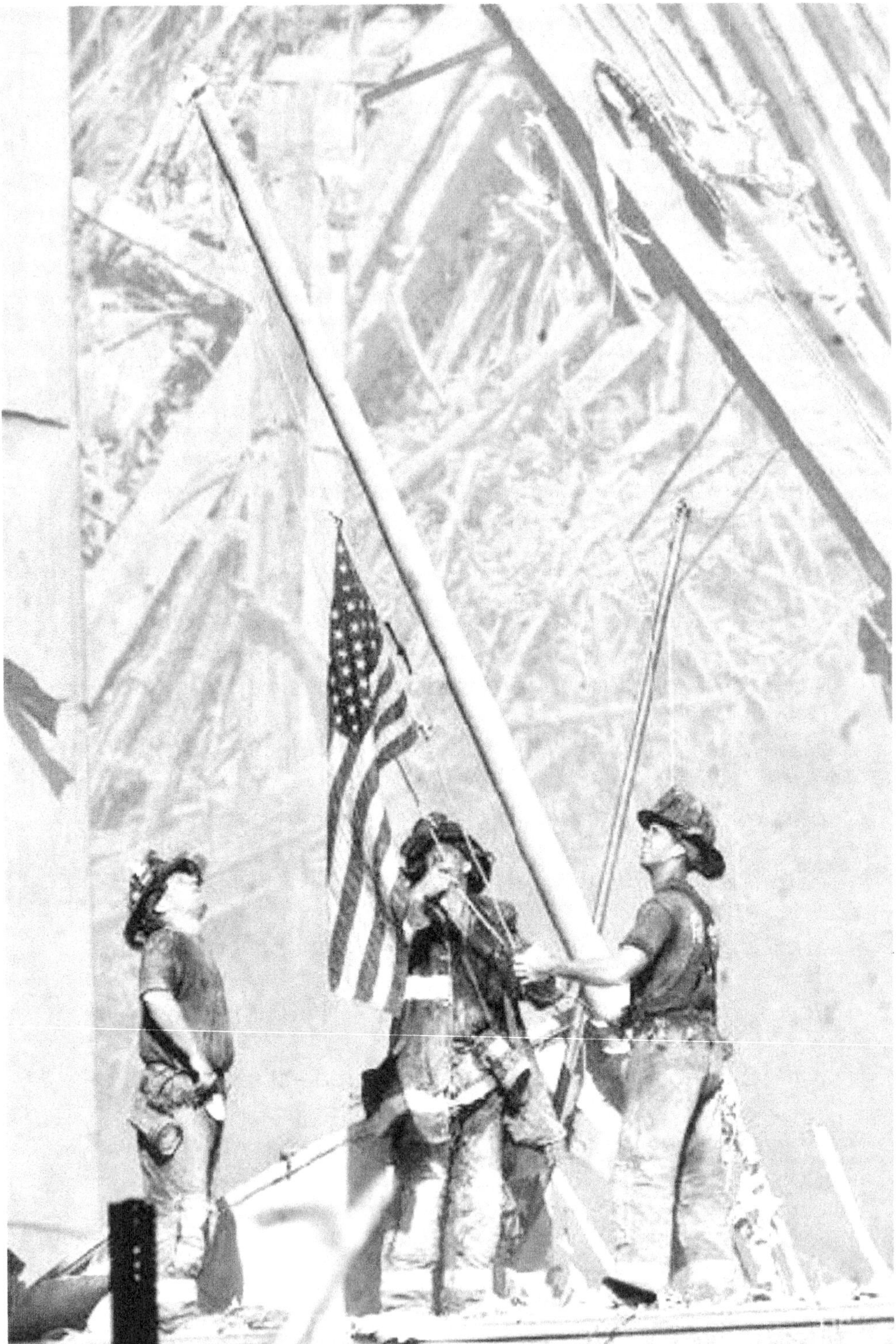

Introduction

Have you ever known in "your knower," deep down inside, something that you can't explain? Like a buoy in the water that keeps bobbin' up and down and won't sink. There's a thought that gets stuck and won't go away. Like, "It's time."

Time for action! Time for change! Time to clean out a crammed closet or change a bad habit. Time to reconcile an estranged relationship. Time to make that dreaded call. Time to say you are sorry or that you were wrong. It's time to change your emotional clothes that carry the smell of smoke and ashes. Time to put on the garments perfumed with praise. Time to mend the mourning and decide to dance again. Time to celebrate what you have and share it with others. Time to refocus on what is important and live like it.

You might be surprised at what the Bible says about this concept called time. The most familiar passage that popped into my head, clamoring for attention, was Ecclesiastes 3:1-8. You know it well: "There is a time and a season for everything," penned by one of the wisest men God created. The thought that had been rolling around in my head did not start there. In my quiet times, the theme the Lord kept speaking about was "it's time." Like a ship cutting through the fog of the night looking for the lighthouse, I could not see clearly what the Lord was saying to me. It became crystal clear while I was listening to Mandisa's song, "He Is With You." [1] The YouTube video painted a vivid picture of where the Lord was directing me. The song begins with the words, "There is a time." Gently, but with great clarity, the Lord was singing His song over my life. The Songwriter's sonata written in my heart that day read, "Come follow me; it's time."

It was one of those moments that compels your heart to say, "Yes, Lord." Go even if your many questions are not yet answered as you step out and into where He is calling you. Fear waves a red flag warning. Danger may be ahead on this journey. Adventure always has an element of danger to it, but so does death! It's a fork in the road you weren't expecting, but one that causes excitement to dance in your heart, even if it is pounding and pulsating throughout your body. It is a time that you do not doubt God but maybe yourself. Wondering, *did I hear Him clearly or correctly*? There are times when we question, "Really, Lord?" Not looking back with so many regrets, nor looking ahead fearing what the future holds in this season of your life, but fully engaged in the path as He goes before you to prepare for such a time as this.

Is it really time, Lord, to see long term prayers answered? Is it time that the ones   prayed for so often will finally find freedom and fulfillment in You? Is it time to step forward in healing and wholeness you have offered for so long? Is it time to see   some miracles after fully believing you could? Will you find it now? Yes, it is time - high time I might - add to wake up to how little time there is left.

Paul threw down the gauntlet in Ephesians 5:16 when he challenged us to redeem the time by "making the most of every opportunity, because the days are evil." The enemy knows our time is short, and we should know it as well. It is time to wake up because what we don't know can and will hurt us. It is time to step up and to step into the destiny for which God has called you. It is time to feel a fresh wind and see a fresh fire consume our soul. It's time to respond to the Audience of One with unashamed abandonment.

There is no life as thrilling and fulfilling as the one to which He calls us. This is the one for which we were placed on planet earth to know. It's time, are you ready? He's calling you to know things you don't. He is calling you to live life on purpose with a   purpose. Join me in exploring the eye openers in Ephesians. He has amazing things ahead and you will need to know. It's time.

Chapter 1

It's Time You Know What You Don't

I feel the heat rising. I sense unfinished business that need to be addressed. I am aware of urgency, not just of age but also of timing.

> *"There is a time and a season for everything under heaven. A time to be born, a time to die. A time to plant and a time to uproot. A time to kill and a time to heal. A time to tear down and a time to build up. A time to weep and a time to laugh." (Ecclesiastes 3: 2-4, NIV)*

This time is different. The heat is rising, the time is short, and there is unfinished business. It is time to discover what I do not know.

How am I to know what I don't? If what I don't know
can hurt me, then how   can I find out? I am a question
asker. When I worked with the doctors in radiology, I
warned them ahead of time. I tend to ask a lot of questions,
not with the intention of irritating them, but to learn. I
realized if I did not fully understand my job then harm
could come to their patients. I developed all the radiology
films for the radiologist, from general X-rays to orthopedic
departments. If I put the wrong name on the wrong film,
the wrong person might get the wrong operation - a worst-
case scenario. Or, the right person might get the wrong
knee operation. I was adamant about my need to ask for
vital information that proved to be very important, at least
to that patient. I had one day of training for this high-
paced, important job. I needed everybody to be patient,
keep their shirts on and give a girl a fighting chance! It
helped to explain to most of the doctors why I did ask so
many questions, but it still irritated some doctors (one, in
particular). The poor fellow had a chip on his shoulder. I
didn't help him, as he saw it, by asking questions. I was
telling everybody to keep their shirts on and telling this
doctor to knock it off – well, at the least the chip. All the
time in between, I was running to the dark room
developing films. In the end, I left that profession and I
went into the counseling field, and then into coaching
where it is my job to ask questions. Although, sometimes it
is still seems irritating asking needful questions to some. I
feel strongly that if you don't get to the heart of the matter,
whether it is with a client or a patient, there won't be
healing.

   Paul was a question asker as well, so at least I am in
good company. He had some critical, life-altering
information that his fellow believers needed to know. In

Ephesians 1:15-21, Paul asked the Lord to do something he could not. It's something no preacher, teacher, counselor, or coach can do either. He started at the right place by asking the right Person to do something so vital that it could change one's whole life. He basically asked for three things: sight, light, and connection. It was so simple, but so profound. Paul was acutely aware that what his readers did not know could hurt them. Hurt them not only if they didn't "get it," but also as they failed to live the very life Christ had died and risen to give them. Not only would it short-circuit their own lives, but it would affect everyone with whom they encountered. It was so crucial that Paul kept asking. That is what persistent prayer looks like. I call it "asking action." You see prayer is the work; everything else is just the outcome of the asking.

When you realize that truth is what you don't know that can and will hurt you, asking is the next step for you. "Ignorance is bliss" is only true if you have dementia or Alzheimer's. I work with this precious population and ignorance is bliss. This disease takes away the identity of a person who suffers with it, but strangely enough, so does not knowing who we are in Christ. It blinds you to your true identity. You live out your life on earth less than God created you in Christ to live. On Judgment Day, the Bema for the believer, the accounting will take place. Not for your sins that were fully paid for on the cross with the cry, "It is finished," but for your rewards and how you invested the life He gave you here on earth.

Paul starts the letter to the Ephesians by asking the Lord through the Holy Spirit to open their eyes. In fact, he asked Him to fully dilate their eyes spiritually. Why? In order that they fully see and understand what their authentic identity is and why it matters so much. He knew they needed to fully grasp in the here and now how completely God had blessed them with everything they needed to live as overcomers. How important is it to know these liberating truths? It is as critical as life and death, victory or defeat, satisfaction or dissatisfaction. What we don't know can and will hurt us!

I love the way Paul jumped immediately in with both feet in Ephesians. He had something so profound and life changing to share, that he burst right through the door praising the God and Father of our Lord Jesus Christ. It was as though he could not get it out fast enough. It was like he had a fire in his bones that prompted him to stand up and shout out, "How great is our God!" The words just tumbled out, referencing what Christ has done for us and in us and in the light of these truths what He wants to do through us. I know that feeling as a teacher. It seems so hot on my tongue, burning in my heart, that I just can't get it out fast enough. Just trying to wrap my mind around His amazing grace, *charis-His favor, benefit, acceptance, or His divine influence on a heart and its reflection in the life.* [1] Or, to communicate the astounding peace, shalom that Paul unites together with grace to sum up all the gifts of Christ. *"This greeting becomes a prayer that the reader may know fully the free, undeserved favour of God, restoring them to Himself, and adding to them all that they need and that they may know the peace with God, peace in their hearts, and peace with one another."*[2]

As a communicator of truth and a learner, I ask the Lord to do what I cannot. I ask Him to open His word, speak the truth, and teach His will and His way. Oh, the power of praise and the penetrating power the Spirit of wisdom and revelation bring! He gives us the inside connection we must have to put the puzzle pieces together in order to really get it.

That's why Paul called it a mystery, *a musterion a previously hidden truth unveiled by God's revelation*[3] in Ephesians 1:9. So what is the secret? What is the big deal? The kind of secrets I usually deal with as a coach and counselor are the kind most families hope won't ever go public. The pink elephant in the room type of secrets so many families experience in life. This secret Paul exposed is a huge deal, and when fully grasped, involves life and death issues. Put more bluntly, it's a heaven and hell truth that hangs in the balance! The big deal for the Old Testament believer was the secret not fully known as the truth was progressively being revealed. The time had not yet come for the whole truth to come to light. They received the promise with a timetable of what was to come and were told to look for it.

It all started in the garden. It was lost in the garden. It caused the fall in the   garden. It was retrieved and restored in a garden., where Christ sweat bullets of blood. Then, there was the shot heard 'round the world: "Not my will, but your will be done" and finally, "It is finished." It will ultimately return to a perfect garden. In the meantime, it took a plan of action that would be so catastrophic that it would cause the earth to shake violently. It would cause the Father's face to be turned away during Christ's darkest moment. It would cause the angels to wonder and weep. Hell and its host would laugh hideously before they realized their real fate according to Colossians 2:15. It would cause the veil in the Holiest of Holies to be torn from top to bottom. Access right into the Presence of God would open. His red carpet of welcome was rolled right out to all people (Hebrews 10:20-22). The shot heard 'round the world is still being heard today. Come see and be saved.

You see, The Fall did not catch the Lord off guard. It did not create for the Creator a "whoops moment." Nor did it cause a "Let us regroup and go to plan B Moment." Nor was redemption an afterthought. According to Ephesians 1:4-14, the Plan of the ages was put into place before the whole thing started at creation. For Christ to give His life as a ransom for those held captive from The Fall, the Three-In-One planned redemption was His purpose (Colossians 1: 1-13).

The Old Testament believers were given a promise as early as Genesis 3:15. A promise was put into motion through a single family, a man named Abraham. The story unfolded as we know it to be; it is His-story. It was walked out through the ages in a promised son foreshadowing the Promised Son and Savior to come. The Old Testament believer saw the shadow; we see the Spotless Lamb of God, who at the right time and in the pre-planned place, came to earth to personally fulfill the promise given long ago (Ephesians 1:10).

It was as if Paul took a telescope and gave us a macro view looking back before the beginning of time. Then he looked forward through to the view of the completed truth under a microscope, right into the present age and the one to come. He throws out truths that theologians – with minds much smarter than mine – wrestle with to this day. Words were included like adoption, predestined, chosen, marked, and sealed. He used words comparing the Holy Spirit to a down payment, a deposit guaranteeing things to come. He planned to bring the Old Testament believers from before the cross and New Testament believers after the cross together under one Head, which is Christ.

The New Testament believers became the church, the body, and the bride of Christ. It would be a story in His-story that would seem too good to believe. Christ gave mankind a new start all over again. What Adam lost in the first garden the second Adam Christ would regain in the second garden and on the cross (Romans 5: 12- 17). Yes, "amazing love, how can it be that you my God would die for me." It still staggers my mind to this day! Another songwriter wrote, "It takes my breath away." This gift keeps on giving. He would unite us with Him as one. Christ's as our husband is now ours. Everything - all of it in Christ - is ours! Inheritance of earthly wealth often breeds family disputes. The inheritance we have in families of origin cannot compare to our inheritance in Him. It starts on Earth, but never ends on Earth or in Heaven. It is ours to draw down from everyday for everything.

Everything lost in Adam has been regained in Christ, plus so much more. That is another book for another time. The sad story, however, is so many don't realize the extent of their inheritance in Christ. They do not know what is in the will. Maybe they haven't even read it in the book. It doesn't take a Philadelphia lawyer (as we say where I came from) to figure it out. But it does take the work of the Holy Spirit to answer Paul's prayer for sight, light, and connection. That is why I am praying for you - that the Holy Spirit will do His best work in you as we walk together through these eye-openers in Ephesians.

You see, the one thing that debates so often cause is division. As I see it, the Lord marked out the course. In His omniscience, He knew ahead of time who would and would not respond to His good news. In giving us a free will, He allows us to make the choice. He moved Heaven and Earth to bring us back into a relationship with Him.

He will never force us! He will woo us and invite us to join Him on the journey. He paid too high a price to leave anyone out. The choice is yours. It's yours for the choosing; it's yours for the losing too, but the invitation is to all. It's time to respond. It is time to know what you don't and to respond to the One who is revealing Himself to you in His word.

I am inviting you to come to my house, in my humble opinion, my mansion. My address is Ephesians 1-6. There are many rooms, space for all of you. You are more than welcome to come, dine, and just move on in with me. You have the red-carpet welcome to come and stay. It was rolled out for me. This grand dwelling was given to me and now to you. It's time to come and stay.

Chapter 2
IT'S TIME TO DECIDE WHICH WORLD

The power of love in the first degree kept pounding in my head as I woke up one morning. I had not even had my first cup of coffee to jump start my day. Murder in the first degree was a familiar term, but what was this "love in the first degree" that called for my attention before my feet hit the floor. I began to engage the thought with visions of the nightly news that screams every night about another murder. Questions are thrown around by the media and those who watch news streaming with clamoring voices: *Was it pre-planned or not? Was it murder in the first degree? Will they get away with it? Will there be enough evidence to convict? Will that individual be found guilty?*

It boggles my mind that anyone would take another human life in a premeditated, willfully planned, and intentional manner! Yes, I studied maladaptive and abnormal behavior in my counseling classes. It still baffles my mind until I consider scripture. I find that the Lord goes directly to the heart of the issue. The mirror of the word lets me see my heart and what horrendous sin I am capable of – as are you. As humans we often think of sins in varying degrees. Some are lesser evil; some are greater evil. We have this internal tape measure that lines up one sin against another, often with "mine is not as bad as the other persons'" comparison. The Word has a way of breaking the ruler of judgment. As God views it, all or any sin would cost the price of redemption, the highest price that ever could or would be paid. He sees it as a thing of the heart before the hands even get involved (Matthew 15: 18-20).

What is in the heart will eventually work its way out in words or wars that affect a home, a community, a place of work, or a place of worship. James 4:1-5 minces no words by stating that murder committed with the mouth, first originates from the heart. James pops off one finger pointing reason after another for the wars and fights we wage in all the arenas we walk into here on Earth. The wars that are within us work themselves outward in words or actions. James names six without blinking an eye. They fall under the umbrellas of uncontrolled pleasures, unfulfilled desires, and ungodly methods to get what we want. James spits them out in rapid succession. We don't pray or we pray with ulterior motives. He does not stop there but continues with unloving attitudes, an uncommitted life, and unclean relationship with the world to boot. These are his assessments of the potential of our hearts if we choose them.

All of us start at the foot of the cross where we realize what we are capable of without the power of deliverance in the resurrection. For any who choose to look out, instead of looking in, we might need to sit down and think about it for a moment. Until we surrender through the means of salvation and daily surrender to the sanctifying work of the Holy Spirit, we won't begin to understand grace. Grace humbles us because it is all of God, and we are just receivers of His mercy. Embrace this thing called grace and you will be humbled and exalted. That's why it is called amazing grace. A multitude of songs and sermons have been birthed from "seeing" the work of grace for the first time or for the umpteenth time.

Not only do we all stand guilty at the cross, but we stand condemned to die under the wrath of God, which is against sin (Ephesians 2:3). He is an awesomely and completely holy God who must condemn sin. It must be punished, paid for, and put away. There was no other way. Before a holy and righteous God, we stood guilty, condemned, under His wrath, without a leg to stand on, and with no way to save ourselves. The gavel heard in the court of sinners cried out "guilty in the first degree!" Death was the sentence handed down. In disbelief, the court stood silent and stunned with what was heard next, "Not guilty!" "His great love for us, rich in mercy, made us alive in Christ even when we were dead in transgressions, it is by grace you have been saved." (Ephesians 2:4)

God's agape love meets our deepest need with our highest interest at heart. Love in action is His goodness, His grace, and His mercy, undeserved, unmerited, and unworthy of us. The old hymn had it right, "Just as I am without one plea." That is LOVE in the first degree. It's a love that is premeditated, willfully planned, and on purpose. Only He did not take a life, but He gave His life and took our place on death row. He gave His life so we could be brought back into relationship with Him. We praise you Lord.

That would be enough to sing His praises forever, but that is just half the truth. As the radio host Paul Harvey used to say, "Let me tell you the rest of the story." That is our ticket out of jail plus it saves us from hell, but we need so much more power to live in this world. Our environment is often toxic and tainted by sin and self-centered living. We need to know and experience the gracious provision God gives us in His Son and the Holy Spirit who lives in us. We need to know that we have a reason to live here on earth with power and purpose. We are called not to dance to the world's ways. We are not to live life from the mindset from which the world would like to squeeze us into living. Finding out who we are in Christ sets us free to embrace life on the horizontal from the vertical perspective. Do not think that finding who we are in Christ is a "self-actualizing" way of thinking. It is not a narcissist train trip to nowhere. It is about being who God created us to be before The Fall. He recreated you in Christ to be here and now. This will be your only path to real fulfillment and satisfaction. It's a path where a life of joy can reign even amid pain. A life lived in freedom and with the fruit of the Spirit in full impact mode. This life is not just about us but about so many more the Lord wants to speak to through our lives and not just our lips.

At a loss for words, Paul strains to convey a truth that takes believing to experience. He called it the incomparable riches of His grace because there is nothing on earth in which it compares. Remember when we talked earlier about everything that is Christ is ours now because of our vital union with Him? Every spiritual blessing is ours in Christ here and now on planet Earth for a reason. Paul unpacks even more of this truth that just gets bigger and better as he opens it up. He reaffirms the truth he has already shared about our union with Christ and the body of Christ. Paul gives an addendum to this revelation. We were also raised with Christ, and we are seated with Him in heavenly realms. Not physically yet. That will happen at the rapture, but it will be in our spirit. Our real life is hidden with Christ in God (Colossians 3:3). Our feet are planted firmly on planet Earth; that does not mean we are too heavenly minded to do any earthly good. Far from it! Instead, it helps us live our life from a whole different perspective and with the power of His life in us.

In our heart there is a strange but real sense that this world is not our home and we are just passing through. Part of His plan is that He wants you to bring others with us.

While we are passing through on this journey there are a few things He wants us to know. Things that will help us choose the world to come, not the world in which we are currently living. You are His workmanship (Ephesians 2:10), *poiema¹* a work of art or a masterpiece. We are His creation, designed with a definite purpose. He is writing the story – a poem – cooperate with Him because others are reading it. Does what others see (or I should say be one who others see) make others thirst to know Him. Are you fully aware and engaged with the purpose and the plan He has put you on planet Earth to fulfill? He has a specific calling on all our lives. He calls us in salvation to come to Him and receive Him. He calls us to worship, to know Him intimately and make Him known. He calls us to allow His life to be lived out in our personalities so that others look at us and see Him. He has a "to do" list of what He is calling us to do which He planned. He gives us a choice to join Him. He gives us gifts and capacities fitted for our calling. In the end, He will give us rewards for what He did in and through us. There is no deal on Earth like this deal in Heaven.

In the closing verses, Paul calls us to remember that we are in a family now, consisting of both Jews and Gentiles. Remember who we used to be when were separated from Christ and Old Testament believers. Now we are saved and set in a family unit. It's a new family that is a global family of all nations and peoples. Our bodies are the temple or the dwelling place of Christ. Maintaining the temple inside and out is your spiritual act of worship. Remember the Head and the cornerstone is Christ alone. Beware of who you are now and of your surroundings. We house the King of Kings and Lord of Lords by His life in you. Live in this world like you belong to the other world. There may be many who will see and believe, many who will be encouraged and inspired by the way you live. We have a world coming called eternity, Heaven, a new earth, and the New Jerusalem. We can relish in the thoughts of things to come. "I can only imagine," as the song goes. (Reference song) He has given us a glimpse in the Book, but it will be more than the eye can take in right now. It's time to choose which world.

CHAPTER 3

IT'S TIME TO CASH IN

Just recently, one of our sons decided to do a family tree search on Ancestry.com. Christy, our daughter, had worked on researching several years back as had our daughter-in-law, Melinda. Each of them found new things about the family from their searches. Having a weird sense of humor, I jokingly said to them, "you might want to be careful; you might find skeletons in the closet." I guess it takes a counselor's mind to process that way, but I have walked into more than a few of those closets with my clients.

Our son, Eric – a financial expert who works with vast numbers – found great joy in letting us in on some family secrets. As he traced both sides of the family back to the 1500's he found records and pictures of a very distant relative near Cary, North Carolina who was quite wealthy. Eric took great delight in sharing every juicy detail with his dad and me. This ancestor had several thousand acres and many hired hands he employed on this large estate he owned. Eric, being a "numbers man," calculated what his estate would be worth in today's market. The amount tallied up to several million dollars. Then with a sheepish grin on his face, Eric informed me, "Looks like you got left out of the will, Mom." As I was working on this manuscript, my mind went back to what Eric said. I smiled sheepishly to myself and thought, *Son, you just don't know I am in the will that matters, and my inheritance in Christ will make my distant cousins look like chum change in God's economy.*

We have never been rich, as this world would define it. I was born in Philadelphia, as was my oldest sister, Sandy. We lived with Grandma Batts in a two-story row house. Daddy was in the Navy for years after we were born. He was a chef and often out at sea. We left Philadelphia when I was two years old to move down south to the little town of Monroe, North Carolina to live with our other Grandma Hinson. Her home was on a farm with several acres and lots of chores to keep us busy. Busy does not equate to happy, so I often found trouble in my boredom and curiosity. My older sister, Sandy, my younger sister, Jan, and I developed a unique sense of humor. They both tended to tell stories about me that strangely, I did not ever recall in the same way they did.

One day when we were all grown up and in our own homes, my older sister's sense of humor just got the best of her. She found a framed Norman Rockwell print that she had purchased with great joy. She hung it right on her living room wall just before you entered her kitchen. It was the perfect place for all to see and to hear the story she loved to tell with this picture. It is a picture of a young girl with a black eye and pigtails sitting outside the principal's office. She is grinning from ear to ear as if to say, "Yes, I won the fight!" In the picture you could see the principal and the teacher through the door that was slightly cracked. The bewildered look on both faces revealed they did not know what to do with this little "troublemaker." My sister made sure everyone knew that little girl was me, and she told this story repeatedly. As a child, I was a tomgirl who did not like to wear dresses, but I did love to climb trees and shoot my BB gun. Think of me as the Annie Oakley of the North Carolina frontier!

We still laugh about how that picture became my inheritance. It now hangs in my home. It is there to remind me that there once was an "old me." What seemed to be the "rascally rabbit" in me, by the grace of God, had to undergo a major do-over. God is the master artist of do-overs. My sisters have been praising the Lord for my do-over for years, but strangely enough, they keep telling the "old me story." Well friends, you are getting your own do-overs, even if they are not quite as dramatic!

We were poor but felt loved. We never lacked for food or clean clothes. We did not have an inside bathroom in the little farmhouse we shared with our grandmother. We slept two to a bed with several quilts in the winter since there was no heat. Needless to say, my older sister never got cold because she kept herself wrapped around me. More than once, I had to get untangled just to breath. I have had to work on separation issues ever since. This is my counselor's confession; please humor me. Our outside facilities consisted of a two-sitter hole in a cute little outhouse. As I am getting older, I wonder what were they thinking? Who wants to be in a two-sitter cute outhouse with anybody? When we moved to the big city of Charlotte, we thought we had died and gone to Heaven. We had an inside bathroom and running water! We were the Clampett's from the Beverly Hillbillies, gone to town. This was fine living, and we assumed we had become rich.

Our Dad was a fun-loving, sanguine sailor before he received Christ at the age of 45. The radical change was like night and day and seemed to happen overnight. His appetite for the Word of God was ravenous. He only had an 8th grade education, but he would do word studies. He would go to Webster Dictionary and later to commentaries to find out the Greek or Hebrew word meanings. What he learned excited him so that he had to share. He became a Sunday School teacher and taught for over fifty years. He did not have a theological degree but loved the Lord and His Word. When Daddy went to be with the Lord, we counted twenty-five people under his teaching ministry had gone into full time Christian service. Before he passed, he told all three of us girls that he did not have an inheritance to leave us, nor a will to be read. He left behind an inheritance that money could not buy. Two valuable gifts he passed on were ones that will last forever – a love for the Word of God and a love for people. We live on our inheritance every day of our lives. As we see it, we are rich beyond belief.

Paul, of the Bible, found himself with the same attitude as he painted a word picture that describes how rich we are. He used a brush full of purples and yellows to create a sense of royalty and joy. He tells the Church of Ephesians his calling to preach the unsearchable riches of Christ (Ephesians 3:8b). It was as though Paul could not wrap his arms (nor his mind) around the vast riches. It was more than just the gospel and all the gifts given, it was Christ Himself. It was like measuring the oceans one teaspoon at a time. Paul had addressed this issue of the gospel being the power of God unto salvation in Romans 1:16. The word used here is the word we use for dynamite.

When we were young and on the farm our Daddy did everything big. He cooked like he was going to feed an army although he was a chef in the Navy. Everyone wanted to come to our house to eat "Papa Batts' food" no matter what he was cooking. Poor Mama never knew who or how many we would be having at the table on any given day. When Daddy decided to have a garden, it had to be big as well. What seemed like at least two acres of plowing and planting became one of our many chores. I hate hoeing to this day. Daddy was a tenacious man who did not let anything get in his way. In order to plant the garden in the spot he had chosen, he had to remove a stump. He went to the Monroe Hardware Store and bought several sticks of dynamite. He came home placed those dynamite sticks in the most strategic places he could figure and strung the line back to the barn. We all fled to behind the shed and peeked around the corner as he lite the fuse. Slowly, but surely, the fire reached the dynamite and *BOOM*! The tree trunk went flying into a thousand pieces. That was over sixty years ago, and I still remember the exhilarating action. When I read verses on the power of the gospel to change people's lives, I literally see the power of dynamite.

The sacred secret that had been hidden since before creation was now being   uncovered and brought to the light for all to see! God's plan for the ages was being opened and unpacked right before our eyes. The unsearchable riches of wisdom and power birthed the church right into existence. The church that had never existed before now proclaimed Christ being born "in us" as New Testament believers. For the Old Testament believer, the Spirit of Christ came upon them for special services and power to accomplish a task He had called them to do. Now because of the cross, the death, burial, resurrection, and ascension, Christ sat down and poured out His Spirit on the day of Pentecost to live right inside the spirit of every born again believer. No wonder Paul called it the unsearchable riches of Christ. There were no adequate words to explain what was being said. Paul almost found himself speechless!

Through Christ's work on the cross he brought the Gentile outsiders and the Jewish insiders together and started a whole new race. The Message Bible expresses it so inclusively. "What I have been calling outsiders and insiders, stand on the same ground before God. They get the same offer, the same help, the same promises in Christ Jesus. The Message is accessible and welcoming to everyone, across the board." That has major global impact stamped all over it. Not only did he create a new race, but He occupied a new place inside the spirit of man to fill and empower him to fulfill his calling on earth.

He revealed His intention through the church. He put on full display for the devil and demons in the aerial atmosphere to see how amazingly redemptive was His plan of salvation (Ephesians 3:10-12). Even the angels wanted to consider this great wonder according to 1 Peter 1:12. The outsiders became insiders! Both Old Testament and New Testament believers were united together in one family. This is the global, inclusive now, new nuclear family formed out of all nations, a plan for all people everywhere. It is so amazing that it evokes a sense of wonder and worship of His grand redemptive plan.

Can I ask you a personal question? When was the last time you were lost in wonder, caught in a childlike awe? Life is tough! Life can be painful. Things didn't turn out like you planned or thought they would. There may be multiple reasons to illicit blame, feel shame, or be bitter. There may be many justifiable causes for anger or wanting revenge for what has been done to you or against you. Some of you may feel jaded, gypped, or short-changed at this moment. You may have experienced broken trust that came with broken promises. Words or actions spouted out from another broken person you thought you could rely on that failed you. I have seen a lot of pain and been in a lot of pain pits with some very precious people. Many of them did not ask for the pain but received it anyway. Some caught in a self-destructive pattern jumped right in with eyes wide open. Others were duped by the devil or betrayed by their own wounded hearts. You may have the right to turn in or turn out but not turn loose. You have the right! You won't find healing, nor will you be made whole. We always have options; some are more difficult than others. We may have been victimized, but we are not victims unless we choose to be. We are set free in Christ to choose, but the choice must be ours.

Life comes with a warning in this fallen world; beware if we do not work through our pain to healing, we will suffer too long and needlessly. If we don't process the feelings and the thoughts, we will get stuck and become lost in our pain, wandering around in circles, aimlessly headed into a deep painful pit of our choosing.

I believe the answer lies in the prayer Paul prays in Ephesians 3:1-20. Paul had suffered unjustly, cruelly, and often for doing what was right. As he sits in his jail cell at Ephesus, he puts his pen to parchment to encourage others with his suffering. He ushers us right into the Presence of the Great Counselor (Isaiah 9:6). The Counselor not only fully understands our pain but help us unpack it and heals us completely of the deepest wounds ever if we let Him. He is also Jehovah Rapha who heals but does not leave us with healed hearts that bear scars. He means to take those scars and tell His-story through them. He is the One to whom you can never say, "You do not understand what was done to me!" Read Isaiah 53:1-12, just for starters. He is the One who is our Great High Priest, who paid for all that sin and pain. The One who with outstretch nail-scarred hands calls us to come and lay our weary head on His broad shoulders. The One who completely understands but paved a way of grace to bring us back to His throne to find grace and mercy in the time of need (Hebrews 4: 15-16). That time is now my friend. It's time ... come.

Paul asked again for the Holy Spirit to do what only He could do, so he prays. He ask for one all-consuming healing, a comprehension of a love that almost defies defining. He brings us face to face with the only safe place, that is, to know this love by experience. This love will not let us go. This love invites us to rest our weary soul and release it to Him. His love seeks us through our pain on purpose to find healing in Him. It's a love that says, "What I do (or allow) now, you do not know or understand now; you will know later" (John 13: 7). This is a love that calls us to trust Him even when we don't understand His ways! That is why it is called a walk of faith that our naked eye or shortsighted perspective often cannot see. A love that can take the broken pieces of our broken lives as we bring it all to Him, can make us whole again (Romans 8:28). He alone can take the ugly and the unnecessary and bring beauty out of our pain. Amazing love!

To aid us in understanding and grasping the love of Christ, Paul resorts to a means of measure, a word picture we need see to experience. It reminds me of the daisy petal game we played when we were kids. You know – you pluck one petal after another guessing, "He loves me; he loves me not." I might say that is our unstable and often painful way to live. We played that game. We danced that dance with many people in life trying to determine who really loves us. As the country girl in me would say, "It ain't no way to live."

Paul lays down the yardstick to measure how wide, how deep, how high and how long is the stable and satisfying love of Christ. Paul crafts this amazing and immeasurable love like a master carpenter. Even with his scholarly mind - trained with his PhD Divinity Degree from the Jerusalem Theological Seminary - he is struggling to adequately convey it. It is something that cannot be measured but must be experienced to even begin to comprehend. Worship that prostrates us in His Presence, face down, awed, lost in wonder, love, and praise is just the beginning. It's like warming up the instruments to play the grand symphony.

Paul patterns this motif of love in a unique but humbling way. In Eugene Peterson's *The Message*, He says it like this, "So here I am, preaching and writing about things that are way over my head, the inexhaustible riches and generosity of Christ. My task is to bring out in the open and make plain what God, who created all this in the first place has been doing in secret and behind the scenes all along." I love this so much because I feel the same way as dear Paul. In just a few verses before this, Paul says, "This is my life work: helping others understand and respond to this Message. It came as a sheer gift to me, a real surprise, God handling all the details." Please excuse Paul and I as we have as we have a personal conversation. I am so with you, brother Paul.

In the verses after Ephesians 3:14-19, he says, "My response is to get down on my knees before the Father, this magnificent Father who parcels out all heaven and earth I ask Him to strengthen you by His Spirit not brute strength but a glorious inner strength that Christ will live in you as you open the door of love, you'll be able to take with all Christians the extravagant dimensions of Christ love. Reach out and experience the breadth, tests its length! Plumb the depths! Rise to the heights! Live full, lives, full in the fullness of God." This was a *rhema* word to me when I read it. It remains my heart cry as the Lord has enlisted all believers into this work as well.

Wow! It makes our feet want to dance and our hands spring up in the air, doesn't it? The Lord has set us free to fill us up, pour us out, and be filled with His Spirit, described in Galatians 5:22-23 as the fruit of the Spirit: love, joy, peace, patience, kindness, faithfulness, gentleness, and self-control. We must be emptied! What fills us controls us. That is a spiritual fact we can take to the everyday-of-life bank. We can learn this truth first hand or by believing what He says and live like it.

To summarize this amazing, awesome truth, Paul takes up his pen one more time with an exclamation mark finish. Lest we think it is up to us to do the work instead of believing and living it out on planet Earth empowered by his Spirit, he smashes that thought. The last verses read like the words of the Hallelujah Chorus. The symphonic crescendo swells to the highest note, "Now to him who is able to do immeasurably more than all we could ask or imagine, according to his power that is at work within us, to him be glory in the church and in Christ Jesus through all generations, forever and ever! Amen!" (Ephesians 3:20-21) I don't know about you but I am on my feet applauding wildly for the Great Conductor of our soul. Thank you Lord! I am asking for an encore as well! I am seeing one because it is time, the time He said it was for me personally.

We are richer than we ever thought we would be. Unlike the things of this world, His inheritance can't be stolen, or taken, or lost. The one down side is that it can be forfeited. We don't use it, and we will lose it. We must understand what is in the will, what is our inherited birthright in Christ. Ask someone who knows; they will be happy to explain it all to you. It is already ours, but we must choose to believe what has been deposited into our spiritual account. We must draw out of it every day if it is going to make any difference in our lives and the lives of others around us. What are you waiting for? It's time to cash in!

Chapter 4

It's Time To Stop Identity Theft

As I prepared to write this chapter, I received a telephone call from my older   sister, Sandy. She was inquiring about the exact day when all three of "the sisters," as we are known, had gone shopping together for Christmas. We have a blast when we get the opportunity to go shopping together and make memories. I told her the   date I recalled. She said, "No it could not have been that day!" I guessed another day. Again, she adamantly stated that was not the day. I wondered if we were playing the Twenty Questions game until I asked, "Why is the exact date so important?" She proceeded to say her credit card account had been hacked that very day, and she had reported it to the bank. The bank immediately shut the account down but not before my sister had paid for several shopping excursions and a nice meal at Chili's Restaurant! Instantly, I saw red! I can get fiery when injustice needs to be confronted. Whoever had messed with my sister would know that it was not going to go unchallenged.

Mom and Dad taught us about the qualities of good character and stealing was not tolerated. Ever since we were little girls, we were taught by example to care for those less fortunate. Mind you, we were poor with no inside toilet, no running water, and no inside plumbing so we took baths in a tin tub from water heated on the stove. We didn't have too far to look to find some measure of poverty, but we always realized that there were others that needed more help than us. We were always glad to lend a hand and to share what we had with others. We grew up in the atmosphere of grace and giving, but there is one thing that can get us riled up and that is when people steal from us. We would willingly and with great joy give you the shirts right off our backs. All you have to do is ask! So, when Sandy's identity had been stolen, I was ready to fight!

We live in a culture and time where we all are subject to the high probability of being hacked. We spend lots of money trying to secure what little we may have to avoid others stealing our identity. It is enough to keep all of us in high anxiety. We can do all we can to be proactive, and then we must leave it in the hands of an all-seeing God.

Identity theft is big business! However, I want to tell you there is a greater identity theft going on right under our noses. We don't seem to have a clue about what is happening, and that is the intent of the thief. Instead of white-collar crime, I want to suggest it is a black-collar crime. It comes from the darkest place ever, and snakes right into our homes and churches. The goal is to keep us so busy we become unaware of what is going on under the radar to those we love. It comes from the scheming mastermind, the father of lies, (John 8: 44), and the great deceiver (Revelation 20:10). The slick strategy originates from the one who comes to steal, kill, and destroy (John 10:10). He is called the angel of light in 2 Corinthians 11:14, who is hard to detach except when the counterfeit is brought to the original Light and exposed. It is time we pull his scheming plots out into the Light of God's Word, and see how to stop identity theft. It's time, here and now!

When I was growing up, in what my teenage children called "The Dark Ages," there was a game show we watched religiously every week. It was called "To Tell The Truth." It aired on television and became a syndication continuing from 1956-1978. The show had a celebrity host with several well-known actors on the panel each week. The lineup would consist of three contestants that would all pose as one person. Questions were asked of all the contestants with the goal of trying to guess which one was telling the truth. The audience tried to detect whom was the real "Joe Smith" and who were the two impersonators. As we watched the show, fierce competition took place in our living room as we sat in front of our black and white TV. As the drama escalated with the audience and we sisters, the host would say, "Will the real so-in-so please stand up?" The audience held their collective breath and so did we. The chairs were scooted back and suddenly, the real so-in-so stood up. Some watching responded, "No way!" "I knew it was that one!" others proudly proclaimed. Of course, hindsight is always 20/20. The show was quite a hit.

So what difference does it make if we know who we really are in Christ or what our true identity is? Chapter 4 is the BOOM to Chapters 1-3! Paul has clearly and methodically laid out who we are in Christ, Whose we are, Who lives in us, and where we are spiritually located while our feet are firmly fixed on the hot pavement of life. Then like the slam-dunk of a basketball into the hoop, Paul challenges us to live in light of who we are now! Paul insists adamantly that we were not meant to be saved and then become stuck! Nor were we meant to be saved and defeated, or saved and unsatisfied, or save and unfulfilled. We were not simply saved to be left on our own to do our best till Jesus comes! We weren't saved to live an unfruitful or unproductive life. If these places are where you find yourself today, you are a victim of identity theft. The enemy has successfully stolen your identity right from underneath your own nose!

I coach some of the dearest people you would ever want to meet. I often hear, "I don't know who I really am anymore." Or I hear, "I want the real me to come back!" I coached a very precious young lady by the name of Carly who said these exact words during our first session. She has given me permission and her blessing to share her story. She is preparing to tell it herself. The Lord is setting up a platform where He is going to tell her redemptive story to all who will be blessed to hear. Her path to freedom was a hard-fought battle, but Carly was ready to do business with the Lord. She did the tough work to find healing and freedom. After I listened to her story the first night, I asked Carly what she wanted to see happen as we walk together out of the darkness. I asked her for three goals. She gave me three, and we worked with them to walk back across the bridge to healing and wholeness. The top goal for Carly was that she would "find the real Carly again." You see Carly's identity had been stolen, and the price she paid was five years of her precious life. After several months of our time together had passed, the real Carly did return and a "new Carly emerged." She is now experiencing the real Carly that the Lord recreated her in Christ to be. The freedom and healing she is experiencing is surprising Carly and her family. They see the redemptive story being rewritten in her life.

I love to witness do-overs taking place in people's lives. It makes me want to stand and shout, "Yes, Lord, you are the King of miracles and I am going to praise you and thank you for it!" The book of Acts is still being written in our day, as the Spirit of God is free to do His amazing work in us in spite of what we've done. It doesn't matter where we have gone or if we have things we thought we were incapable of doing; He can meet us where we are and walk us right back to freedom, just like He did with Carly! She found the anchor and love of her life. She found the only One that can meet the deepest need of her heart. Carly is a trophy of God's grace.

So often we get lost in our pain, problems, or unhealthy relationships that we lose our God-given identity. Call it enmeshment, call it codependency, call it crazy, but call it what it really is – identity theft. The Fall caused quite an effect. It precipitated a ripple effect that is still being felt right into our current culture. So intently so, that we have learned to build our identity on a crumbling wall and shifting sand that is talked about in the gospel of Matthew 7:24-27. We have repeated this pattern, this cycle, ever since. I call it curse-filled-living, where the   curse keeps giving right into our families, neighborhoods, work places, and places of worship. There are generational strongholds that often fly under the radar if they are not recognized. They become undetected in our families whether they seem "clean or dirty." Either way they divide and destroy relationships in such painful and tearing ways. It was not meant to be this way. There is a way out and strongholds can be broken to the glory of God. I am living proof.

So often we ask the wrong questions of our children. Ones like *what do you want to be when you grow up?* I am all for planning and executing all the education needed to fulfill the God-given destiny for our lives. We need to train and accomplish the skills needed to perform our task or jobs to which God has called us to, whether we become doctors or a stay-at-home moms, but hear this clearly ... that is not our identity! We don't do our children any service if we encourage them to build their identity around shifting sand or on a wall that can crumble, such as a career.

The Lord has placed me in His plans and in many places not in my plans. I didn't understand the curves and courses I would travel over the years of my life. I have worked in many industries from day care to gerontology and everything in between. I never longed to be a jack-of-all-trades but wanted to be a master of one. I went back to college in my 40's and graduated with my Bachelor of Science when I was 50 years old. I was the oldest person in all my classes. That was intimidating much of the time. I began to realize God had me there, and He had me there with a purpose beyond what I could see at that moment. The kids rallied around me as they began to realize I was there for a reason, and my Mom and Dad were not paying my way through college, I was! I was amazed at the opportunities that came for me to share Christ with the younger students during their crises. When there were group projects, they all made a beeline to me, knowing they were going to have to carry their fair-share load for the team. Clear boundaries were set about what they had to do to keep our group grade on an A standard. Often these students were aware of the battles I had gone through, yet they also saw my joy. They asked me how I could be so "happy" with so much against me. Well, that was a loaded question with a wide-open platform to walk them right to Jesus.

When I went back to college, my identity did not rise or fall with my profession. If it had then when I was almost finished with my Masters of Christian Counseling at a well-known seminary, it would have crushed me. I had to take a time-out when I was within four classes of being finished with the program. We had several deaths during this time - one being my mom's, which was very difficult to handle. I experienced several months of grieving, and depression was my companion. Difficulties at home and working full-time had taken their toll on my body. I tried to return a few years later only to be told I would need to start all over again. Sadly, after years of studying and spending a lot of money, this journey had come to an end. It was hard to deal with, but I realized that was not my identity and went forward, asking *what do I do now Lord*?

I went to work at a wonderful assisted living center where life was respected and dignified as a ministry to our senior citizens. I had the privilege of teaching these precious people Bible Studies every week for eighteen years. I became an anchor for these dear folks in the greatest transition of their lives. Old age is difficult. I also had the honor to work with young couples struggling in their marriages, with people going through midlife crises, and with others who were becoming empty nesters. I had the great joy of teaching in my local church. Ministry and work were always there; I just needed to walk one step at a time where the Lord placed me and with the people He sent me. I am a mutt, and I am ok with that. My identity lies in my relationship with my Creator and Redeemer who knows where He was taking me and why. I learned to rest in Him and find my greatest fulfillment in the love relationship that He would develop in me as my true identity.

Let me ask you a very personal question. *To what is your identity hooked?* Which basket holds all your eggs? The world trains us to hang our hats on the three B's- beauty, brains, and bank accounts. If you have any or all of these, try to hold on and keep them from slipping through your fingers. Are you climbing that ladder of success to get what you think will make you happy and fulfilled? Let me speak a warning – you are building your life on shifting sand. The valid and revealing truth is that the only stable, satisfying, and fulfilling identity is found it Christ alone. The sad reality is we often find this out only after we have run so hard after everything but Him. Maybe you are feeling like Humpty Dumpty in your life right now. You know the children's nursery rhyme. Humpty Dumpty sat on a wall. Humpty Dumpty had a great fall. All the king's horses and all the king's men could not put Humpty Dumpty back together again. The question that rhyme is meant to evoke in the children who read it is *why*? You know the answer. Humpty Dumpty was an egg and he broke all to pieces. It's a sad story and an unfortunate ending to such a good egg, right? Even if your life feels broken and disappointing right now, the amazing call comes from the greatest Healer. He can take all your broken pieces and make something more beautiful than you could ever imagine. Bring your broken pieces; let Him show you the "real you," your true identity, the one He created.

I absolutely love how Paul burst the bubble of babbling we often get caught in as the great deceiver seeks to weave lies to trap us in his web. And oh the webs we do weave when we seek to be deceitful. In Ephesians 1, the *Message Bible* says, "It is in Christ we find out who we are and what we are living for." Have you discovered this whether young or old? When I read this in scripture, I see in my artistic mind the black birdcage on my back porch. The cage is open and empty. The door is wide open, and I like it that way. It is amazing I have never seen a bird try to get into that cage even with the door open and accessible. They have made nests in every corner of my back porch but have never chosen to have their baby birds born in the cage. I have seen a time when a bird has been trapped in a cage for years and then the door is left open. What puzzled me is the bird chose to stay in the cage. Freedom is right in the bird's reach, and the bird stays in captivity. That sweet bird could go to the bird counselor or rearrange the cage to make it cozier and not so cramped. That little birdie could sing all day long about the freedom outside that door but will not fly through the open space provided. We are a lot like that little bird. At the cross and resurrection, the captives were set free according to Ephesians 4:4. We so often don't realize the door is open or we choose, for whatever reason, to stay in captivity when in reality we have been set free. Why would we remain in captivity? This is not what Christ died to give us!

Paul brings us back to reality by telling us that because we are free, we are to live a life worthy of the high and holy calling we were born to live in Christ (Ephesian 4:1). We have a calling and it is not a self-centered existence, satisfied with just getting by with no impact in this life for the King and His Kingdom. Oh no! Paul tells us He has a specific plan for every one of our lives. We live in community and we function as a family. Paul challenges his fellow believers to move into action and not to be content to sit on our hands. He says, "I am locked up like a bird in a cage but free in the Spirit to use the gifts of writing and encouraging." Preaching behind bars seemed to be a specialty of Paul's since every time he turned around they threw him back in jail. This was one jailbird that was not singing the blues. His cage could not contain his spirit, because he knew who he was in Christ and he was singing it out to everyone who would listen.

In fact, Paul testified that his chains were being used to advance the gospel in Philippians 1:12-14. His chains and his cage were not the end of his ministry. They were just the launching pad to shoot out the arrows of truth, to set other captives free that were not behind physical bars. What Satan meant for evil, God used for good through Paul. Paul was bound physically but was spiritually "free in Christ." This jailbird spoke freer in jail than he ever could if he were free outside the jail.   You and I have the benefit of the Spirit because of what the Lord was free to do in and through Paul. That is so encouraging to me! What chains or cells do you find yourself in today? Are you confined in a cage of illness, relational difficulty, or financially chains, caught in an endless cycle of trying to get free? How are you responding to your chains? What is the Lord trying to set you free from? Is the Spirit of the Lord free in these situations to minister to others?

Paul pulls no punches as to how they are now to live in community as well as outside the doors of the church to the reach the needy on the other side of the walls. He calls us to realize as we are in community where others are watching us as a body of believers now called the church. He gives us a sevenfold reason. We have unity in the body, and we are called to pay attention and make every effort to keep the unity. It does not matter to which denomination you hook your wagon, but this is what unites us across denominational lines. I find it amazing he says one, one, one, over and over again. One body, one Spirit, one hope, one Lord, one faith, one baptism and one God and Father of all, who is over all, through all, and in all. This is what and who unites us, so don't let anything else divide us. That is clear. If there is a problem, please take it up with the Lord, or you might be one who is causing the division.

To all believers the Spirit of God gives gifts to each to fulfill His calling in our lives. It is to build up the body to function as a healthy body. It is not to make the gifts a point of contention of who is great and who is not. When it does, we have missed the whole point. He calls some of us as preachers, evangelists, and teachers to equip the body of Christ to minister to the multitudes in salvation or sanctification. His aim is that we be built up and not be tossed about with every wind of doctrine that is not biblical and balanced, lest we get off course according to Ephesians 4:10-16. This is His instruction to us corporately; it's one with the call to hear and heed.

Then Paul brings it home in a downright personal way in verses 17-32. He lays out what will steal our true identity if we don't see it and stop it. He reminds us that   some things don't fit who we are in Christ and must be put away. In fact, he uses the analogy of taking off the old self and putting on the new self. The old self, or our old identity, revolved around us. The old self, or our flesh, is the way we learned to cope or compensate for what came your way in life, good or bad. The new you is who you really are, as you are born again, and the Spirit of God takes up residence in your spirit. This happens, in part, through the renewing of your mind (Romans 12: 1-2). He begins to change you from the inside out as you cooperate with His leading. He will set you free to be who He created you to be. This is life, life in the fullest sense.

In rapid succession, Paul throws out what this looks like in everyday life on planet Earth where it can be downright difficult and next to impossible. The good news is He never called you to do this on your own but with and through the Living Victorious Christ who lives in you by His Spirit. You are His vessel if you will let Him live through you.

No more lies; tell the truth. Be angry but don't sin in your anger. Be angry over the right thing in the right way. Deal with it before you go to bed; unresolved anger does not make for a good bed partner. Leave revenge to the One who can do it justly and with mercy and grace. Don't steal but work so you can pay your bills and help others in need. Watch your words; they are weighty, so weigh them before you say them. Words can start fights and wars or bring comfort and healing. Remember what is in the heart has a way of working out in actions and attitudes, not in alignment of who we are now. Don't give the Devil a foot in the door for he is more than happy for us to give him an inch. He will take the inch and push for a mile. Don't be our own worst enemy. Don't grieve the Spirit. He is a person - the third Person of the trinity. He is God! He loves us and we can misunderstand that love with selfish thoughts, motives, and actions. He lives in us to help us. Do not hinder His work in you. Stop backbiting. Be the same in the front as you are in the back. Authenticity is so winsome and draws others to the living Christ in us. Don't give others a wrong picture of the precious and powerful God who lives in us. Forgive, not because they deserve it (neither did we), but because God forgave us and continues to on a daily basis. Forgiveness sets us free. Set the Spirit free to do what only he can do. Let Him do it. He is God and we are not! The Spirit is our indwelling alarm detector listen to Him.

It is time we stop identity theft! Know who you are in Christ. Only you can stop identity theft in your own life. When you do then you have the freedom to speak it into someone else's life. It's time!

CHAPTER 5

IT'S TIME TO REALIZE SOME THINGS DON'T FIT

It was May of 2000, right before I graduated from Gardner Webb University. I was finishing my finals, and I was so ready to graduate. I was doing my internship for my Counseling degree with a Christian Counseling group called Women at The Well. I enjoyed working with two very godly and wise licensed counselors. We were doing a pilot program, one of the first in Charlotte. We handpicked twelve young women who had been in counseling for some time. Each one had experienced some very painful traumas in their lives. Some of the sweet ladies had been sexually molested and others verbally and physically abused. All of the girls were believers. Elizabeth and Barbara asked me to accompany them on this weekend retreat.

We went to the old PTL campus (Jim and Tammy Bakker's ministry) in South Carolina where we camped out for the night. I was so sick, but I was determined not to miss this opportunity. To watch two very gifted ladies work with some of the most difficult cases we had in the practice, was a dream come true. It was called "Intensive Care." The ministry of intercessory prayer and Biblical truths were preparation for the transformation we longed to see take place. We created a safe place where the girls could be open, vulnerable, and authentic. The environment of love, acceptance, and grace gave the Holy Spirit a clean atmosphere to work deep down inside and to bring healing. He came with tenderness but in power that day to heal the brokenhearted!

If you have not experienced this kind of pain, it is hard to identify with those who have lived through devastating circumstances like these. Each lady had made a profession of faith and experienced new life in Christ. How do you reprogram the mind? How do you begin to teach ladies, who see themselves as "damaged goods," who they really are in Christ? Good questions. There is no pat answer and one size does not fit all. What I did discover was the critical role a grace-filled counselor or coach has in facilitating the healing process. The great Counselor lives inside us. He is there to speak healing into the hearts of those shattered by the sin. There is good news, oh yes! It is desperately needed and provided by the Sovereign God of the universe who spoke and the worlds came into existence. He comes to heal the brokenhearted.

These precious ladies heard the truth and received the Word of freedom that   you are reading in this book. The Son came and the Son spoke! When the Son sets you free, you are free indeed (John 8:32)! We praise you Lord! Many of the trophies of His grace and mercy serve in our churches to this day. You may never know it   unless they share it. You may be sitting by one of these ladies this Sunday. You see healing and beauty go together! The radiance of Christ can outshine the darkest days or devastation in anyone's life. He came to set the captive free. He came to heal the brokenhearted. He does just what He says He will do (Luke 4:18).

Sometimes our addicted friends walking this freedom out on a daily basis are wiser than we are. Those of us who live and walk in a "cleaner" environment take for granted what they know and live as the gospel truth. In order to get free and stay free we have got to do serious business with some important matters in our life. The path back to the pit is only inches behind us. It does matter where our thoughts take us. It most certainly matters what company we keep. It does matter that we take a ruthless inventory of what we are allowing into our lives. They know defeat is only a thought away. They also know at all cost they do not want to go back! So, they deal with their issues daily. How about you? We might be freer if we follow our sweet friends' examples. Pride blinds us but sweet grace humbles us. It sets us free. Come and see!

It's time to be emptied out and time to be filled up. It's time to be opened up, and it's time to be healed up. It's been way too long letting these chains bind us. It is time to empty out the years of infection that lie within us, allowing the skilled surgeon to lance the wound and then let Him stitch us back together again. There will be scars, but as Mandisa sings, "scars aren't pretty but they are a part of me." They are a reminder of His faithfulness. I sing *That's What Scars Are For*[1] with great joy right along with Mandisa, celebrating fresh victories over the sin that tries to cripple.

Some things don't fit anymore. It is time to decide what does not fit in our new life in Christ. The Word says when we are born again, the very life of Christ is birthed right into our dead spirits, quickening our spirit to life (Ephesians 2:1).

Old things pass away and all things become new, 2 Corinthians 5:17 tells us. We were once children of darkness; now we are children of light (Ephesians 5:6). The Spirit of Christ comes to live in us, as John 14: 17 says, to teach us, counsel us, and testify to all.

Paul invites us to come and dine with our beloved in a command performance. Hang tight by keeping close to him. "Keep company with him and learn a life of love." Observe how Christ loved us. His love was not cautious but extravagant. He didn't love in order to get something from us but to give everything of himself to us." (*The Message*) Love in action fits who we are now – children of God. Living in His light and His love is the starting point for a healthy and whole Christian life. His love heals, forgives, restores, and redeems our sorrows, while setting our feet on the path of freedom to walk with our "Only Savior," ministering to others.

Paul calls us to wake up and realize to whom we belong. *The Message* implores us, "Wake up from your sleep. Climb out of your coffin." Strong words with a strong message! I think he struck a chord we need to pay attention to. We can be wide-awake and sound asleep at the same time. Play on words you might ask? No, it is too often our reality even as believers whose hearts burn for Jesus. It could be something as simple as missing our times alone with Him that restores our souls. He waits every day to meet us and enjoy our company, and perhaps we don't show up. When we do carve out these moments, they are so worth it. Just to be in His Presence fills us up and satisfies the deepest longings of our heart. There are also those times that others are so aware of as they are witness to the "shining face" of one who has been with the lover of her soul. One day missed can become two and maybe then a week will go by. Oh, I have been there with a schedule of kids or deadlines. When you sit down, they stand up and shout at you. The "to do list" that just had sixteen more things added to it. The forever juggling of time with family, ministry, and work meets you. I never wanted to be superwoman, but oh my, most ladies in our culture get shoved right into that role. Until we, by the grace of God and the power of the Holy Spirit, learn to set boundaries and balances that will help us keep our sanity. A side effect of being in balance is that we are easier to be get along with.

As a recovering "people pleaser," the Lord is teaching me a sign language that is working wonders in my life. I have a red stop sign I can show so graciously. If that doesn't work after a few times then a tougher stance may be called for as I just spit it right out, "sit down!" I practiced it the other day when my sweet dog Gibby, an Australian Sheep Herder, had just herded me to the gate. My husband was in his "herding me" mode that day as well, and I had had enough! I turned to Gibby very sternly, and said, "Stop!" My red stop sign face clearly showed that I meant what I said! To my husband, I said the same, "Sit down." I am a grown woman, and I can do it! There is a family fight aired in public. I had done what he has so graciously in protection told me to do. I told him I had followed all his instructions. but he just needed to herd me, and I was not in the "mood" to be herded. You may have had those days as well; I understand. Help me Lord, and they are both males. Just saying; no condemnation, my brothers!

Paul writes one clear instruction after another as he clearly paints a very pointed picture of what does not fit in our lives as children of love and light. As a coach I am going to ask you to read this in an "exercise or assignment" mindset. Sit down and let's process this in a very practical way. Why? We have a very personal Lord who lives within us to be all we need in this transformation. Do not be mistaken, for we also have a personal enemy who is bent on stopping us. If our enemy can keep us in the dark of who we are in Christ, he wins. He can be subtle in his temptations or down right dirty. Whatever works is his philosophy. "All is fair in love and war" is painted right on the wall of his hideous mind. If he can keep us thinking foggy or fuzzy then he wins. His strategy is to keep us from seeing clearly who we are in Christ. He knows why it does make such a huge difference in this life and the next. He realizes that if he can keep us living on the horizontal without living from the vertical he has established a beachhead in our lives that will affect our children. In fact, it will affect generations to come unless we let the Lord blow the lid right off his crafty cart.

As wonderful as the plan and purpose the Lord has for your life is, the enemy's plan is to divide and destroy every time. He knows time is short and he has cranked up his demolition tanks. Just look at the culture around us. Sweet ones, he means business, and we better mean business as well. His tailor-made plan for our family members and the global family is very precise to each individual's own personalities, strengths or weaknesses. He has a laser target ready to send a cruise missile at just the right time and in the right place. Do not be a causality of war, God is on our side and has provided all we need to protect us, but we must take it up and put on the armor. We must know now what does not fit in with who we are in Christ. If we don't, we will aid the enemy. He is not playing games with us or our family. Stop saying life's not fair. When we do, we step right in his devilish den. Of course, it is not fair! Remember his motto: "All is fair in love and war." Additionally, need I add that the prayers to stop him cannot be the type like "Now I lay be down to sleep?" He laughs hideously at the simplistic mindset that a prayer a day will keep the devil away. Oh no, Ephesians 6 tells us plainly that we are at war now with the powers of darkness. We are not ignorant of his devices, but we do not have to fear. We do have to be in our armor, walking in victory over our own flesh and knowing who we are in Christ.

My life's message has been taught on several occasions. This battle was learned   a very hard way on the playing field of life. What I share about my life has blood and pain on it. As long as the Lord gives me the strength and opportunity, I will speak it one-on-one or to the multitudes. The message not only holds weight but brings victory when applied. Know your God, know yourself, know your enemy, and know your weapons – in that order. Learn from an old soldier. It may spare you some awful grief to come!

Paul pulls the partners of darkness right out of the closet in Ephesians 5:3-17. Read it and read it again. This is where the enemy will set the trap. This is where he will appeal to our own flesh flavor. It's coming right at us every day. Counteract that attack! It is our blood-bought inheritance as a child of love and light. Don't help the enemy out! Ephesians 4: 17 has already provided the truth that we can give the devil a place of occupation in our life. He cannot mess with our spirit the dwelling place of the Most High God. He can, however, try to mess with your soul, your mind, your emotions, and your will. This is our soul that is being sanctified by the Spirit of God and by the word of God. We must know who we are and live it out.

When the Lord gives a list of sins it is not to make us sin conscious but to make   us aware of the potential for the enemy to defeat us right inside our heads and out through our bodies. Make no mistake! The enemy is defeated and the enemy has no power or right in our lives unless we give it to him. I cannot say it loud enough or long enough. My ministry is to teach the truth of God's word and to work with precious people who don't know who they are in Christ. Often, I am walking with them out of their own pain or pain others have caused in their lives. Oh, precious one, even if you have been duped by the devil, or willfully walked right into his den, it is never too late to get out of that pit. Never! I am a released POW. As my hero of the faith, Corrie Ten Boom, said, "There is no hole so deep the love of God is not deeper still." It's time to come out!

You might be saying, "Carolyn, give me some practical ways to do this!" I am glad you asked. Here are some brief and direct ways. You don't need a whole list of things "to do" when you are tired already. Ephesians 5:18 tells us to be filled with the Holy Spirit. He is God and the third person of the Trinity. He is the Spirit of Christ. He is your internal power source. What fills us controls us. If we are full of jealousy, anger, rage, bitterness, or unwholesome words, they are what control our thinking and acting. Stop it! In the power of the Holy Spirit, I say no more! Self-pity, self-blame, shame, and all the "we should haves'" we hear in our head stop now! The enemy will come to us in the voice of the "first person singular," and it will be almost impossible to tell if they are his thoughts or ours. In the end it does not matter. Don't spend your valuable energy and time to "discern it." I had a very wise and godly counselor at CPCC who made a statement that has stuck with me for years. He said, "Don't let anyone 'should' on you and don't you 'should' on anyone else." Make sure you read that again. When I say it with my Yankee speed and my southern drawl it sounds like something I did not say. Rewind and reread that statement. It will set you free one day and set others free should you speak unkindly in a way that was meant by the enemy to take you down. I can choose to push it down inside which costs me physically and psychologically, or I can let it fly right out of my mouth in "I have a right, current cultural mentality," poisoning all around me. Hard to live by and hard to deal with, but we have a choice to control our tongue.

When I was doing my Masters of Christian Counseling at Gordon-Conwell Theological Seminary, I had to read and write a lot. One of my favorite writers was Dr. Gary Collins. His book, *Family Shock*[2] was both powerful and painful to read. His subtitle was, "How to keep families strong in the midst of earthshaking change." It was both depressing statistically, but inspiring with answers to the problems we face. Unfortunately, I knew much of his statistics first-hand. My sisters and I had a precious dad who was fun loving, but an alcoholic before he was amazingly saved at age forty-five. His transformation was nothing short of a miracle. He laid the bottle down and, shortly after, the cigarettes as well. Prior to his salvation experience, we would play the game of hiding the bottle in the shed upstairs. Sandy, Jan, and I would go to Charlotte with him and on the way back through Mint Hill, we would always stop at Penny's Tavern which is still stands to this day. He would get an alcoholic drink and bribe us with a Coke if we would not go home and tell Momma. We enjoyed that Coke,. It was so cold and good, but we did not hold up our part of the bargain as we all jumped out of the car running to tell Momma. It is family tensions like these that tear at our loyalty between one parent or the other.

I married into an alcoholic family. Sound familiar? All the stuff and brokenness that trails behind, showing up and sounding off when you least expect it. Playing out in unexpected times and irrational ways when you want to say, "sit down and be quiet", but it won't. How do I set healthy boundaries and what does healthy love really look like? I grew up with the internalized lies and assumed roles to keep the peace or keep the pain down. I acquired internalized lies about God, self, and others that seemed balanced until I received healing and the dance had to change. The thoughts, like trash piling up on the curb, held me captive so long. But then God showed up. Life cannot be the same ever again if you want to cooperate with Him. I did! I did the hard work. In fact, I am still doing it. It is called "renewing my mind." It is a job where the work starts on the inside and is ours for the choosing. It entails taking every thought captive as 2 Corinthians 10:3-5 lays out. I'm guessing you are thinking that sounds like a lot of work! I am here to tell you, my friend, that it is freedom. This bird is out of the cage, and by the grace of God, I am not going back. The option for you or your children may be to come to see people like me to help you get free. I will be there for you, but it is so much better to be proactive. It cost so much less that way. By God's design, pain can be avoided, and precious time and energy to deal with it can be saved. It's time to deal with it, my friend. He paid too high a price for you to remain in your current state of being.

Paul closes the chapter with some overarching principles that can be so freeing if we follow the Book. If we are filled and controlled by the Holy Spirit, this is a glimpse of what it will look like on the hot pavement of life. Wives filled with the Spirit can be healthy and whole in submission without becoming a doormat. We can respect our mate and submit but with input into matters of the home and the children. Husbands filled with God's spirit will love their wives like Christ loved the church and gave Himself for it. Husbands filled with the Holy Spirit and in submission to the Lord can be men of grace and mercy. This will temper their needs to dominate or dictate. As I counsel or coach couples, I take my own counsel since it is in the Book. It takes two people. If your marriage becomes one-sided, here's the deal: it will take the filling of the Holy Spirit and godly counsel to guide you through at times, shark infested waters. Trust God on this one, and if you don't see it this way take it up with God. You may not know the whole story. Maybe they are there out of no fault of their own. Until we can pray for our dear couples with the love of Christ and the filling of the Spirit, we might want to sit this conversation out. Words carry weight. Weigh them out with God before you let them out in the air. Encouraging and instructive words are what do fit who we are in Christ. Please share them often and bathed in His love.

It's time to decide what belongs in my life. It's time to realize some things don't fit. Put out the things that do not belong and pull close those that belong. Be filled and controlled by the Holy Spirit. He makes all the difference in the world.

CHAPTER 6

YOU'RE IN THE FIGHT OF YOUR LIFE

It was the day America went on lock down. We know it as 9/11, the day that changed America forever! In fact, this day changed the world forever. History was marked at that critical, pivotal point in time. From that point forward, time became knows as post 9/11. Uncertainty reigned as America was put on red alert in every area of our lives. War came right into our homes, neighborhoods, schools, and even our very country. Terrorists won the attention of the whole world as we watched, stunned in horror, as the first plane flew right into Twin Tower One. Shocked beyond belief, not knowing what happened, we were glued to our TV's as "Breaking News" interrupted regularly scheduled programs and our very existence!

The words whispered by the Secret Service to President Bush that day brought swift reaction. We tried to grasp collectively as a nation, to make sense of what just happened. It was only the beginning. Twin Tower Two was hit with another strategically aimed airplane much like a heat seeking missile. The tall structure collapsed like a deck of cards. The Pentagon was attacked in a well-orchestrated plan to blow America right off her feet, and it did!

The News Reporters could not report the rapidly changing news fast enough. What in the world was going on? The Twin Towers became flaming infernos as people jumped out of windows to escape being burned alive. We watched in absolute horror and disbelief! Billows of smoke and debris engulfed New York City streets, rolling down them like a smoking tsunami. New Yorkers, covered in ash and debris, ran for their lives. Twin Tower One collapsed and then Twin Tower Two folded. What might have been thought impossible or unthinkable before, became our living nightmare! This was America's and the world's new reality. The attack on our soil united us in a way we had never before been united. Sad to say we have never been as united since that time.

This war became very personal to our nation as some 3,000 Americans lost their lives that day. Families were torn apart as their loved ones died in those towering furnaces. The toll taken on lives would not stop there or on that day, but it would continue for many years to come. For our family, it became deeply personal. Our daughter, Christy, one of the most compassionate people I know, went to New York only days after 9/11. She joined a company to help in the massive and overwhelming recovery of bodies and clean up. She worked beside some of New York's bravest and finest fire fighters and first responders. Their job was to find, recover, and identify the bodies of those who never knew what hit them. As a result of this terrorist attack, she (along with the people of New York) laid eyes on things they should never of had to see or experience. Christy saw things that still haunt her seventeen years later. Sometimes if things don't move us personally, they do not move us powerfully.

The moving of the rubble, unearthing what was left of the body parts, became an arduous and painstaking process. Christy watched as the fire fighters worked eighteen-hour shifts. They refused to go home to their own comfortable beds, and they laid their weary heads on their fire equipment to catch a few hours' rest. Then, they would get right back up and go back into the collapsed towers. Time was urgent and there was so much to accomplish. Christy's senses were assaulted with the smells and the sight of families wandering the streets near the carnage. Many were holding or posting pictures of their loved ones, pleading for someone to help them find their family member. She has always had such a tender heart and been quick to help anyone in need despite what it would cost her. She had been her Momma's lifesaver, often caring for her younger brothers, especially when they came two at a time!

Christy walked the streets of New York with the looming darkness and   unfathomable grief that follows such devastation. She had inside information, much of which most Americans weren't privy. Plans for more attacks existed and were ready to roll on queue. There were plans to come over the bridge and through the tunnels to flood the city. There were plans to finish the job the terrorists had started. Danger ran high and vigilance even higher. She rode the subway very aware of her surroundings and not sure whom to trust.

Christy is a graphic artist by gifting and by trade. She was an entrepreneur with her own very successful business before a devastating relationship destroyed it to pieces. She was on the heels of reeling from her own personal pain when she chose to help others caught in destruction. She is gifted in writing and drawing. She picked up her pen and wrote what she saw all around her. It was her way of processing her pain and entering into the pain of those cherished people in New York. She was so profoundly shaken by what she experienced, she had to put her thoughts down on paper in a poem. Trust, safety, or living life as usual, would never be embraced again in the face of such horror. As I read the poem, I felt the darkness in what was New York's and America's darkest hour.

After the work was finished, Christy returned home, but she was changed forever. In the days post 9/11 and as the aftermath of medical issues began to surface, fire fighters and first responders began to get very sick and died. All had inhaled powdered glass, powdered asbestos, and many other impurities from the Twin Towers' collapse. When the tragic event unfolded, no one had been instructed to protect themselves with masks. Hospital doctors and staff began to see a pattern developing in all the patients' cases. Esophageal cancer, multiple pulmonary issues and emphysema appeared in most of the cases. Post Trauma Syndrome Disorder was widely diagnosed with the fire fighters and first responders. Most toxic of all   was the effect on the souls of our country that had just been attacked.

Christy continued to watch the news religiously as she was suffering with all   these issues as well. She sought out multiple doctors and started taking medication to deal with her many illnesses. She was in a fight for her life, as were the other heroes and helpers. Christy was dying while she was living. She read all the research and followed all the reports that came out of New York. In the months and years following, she felt like the "dead man (woman) walking" with the sentence of death hanging over her head.

This was the world 9/11 had created. America came front and center with a war that was very real and would not go away. As believers we are in a war now with the spiritual forces at work in our world today. Although it is unseen, it is most   definitely very real. The evidence leaves a trail behind that we need to face head on if we are to win this war. This war will never go away according to 2 Timothy 3:1-5. We are actually told it will escalate and intensify and we should be aware and prepare. It will come right into our homes, neighborhoods, work places, places of worship, and our world. It will be finished forever after the rapture and return to the new heavens and the new earth.

This is not to scare us but to prepare us as Revelation 1:1-3 explains. It is to   toughen us and train us as good soldiers of Jesus Christ. It is to awaken and shake us loose from anything that holds us earth-bound. Anything or anyone that keeps us   from being fully engaged in our walk with the Lord needs to be addressed and put in the proper place. We are called and challenged to our birthright as victors and not victims or causalities of this war.

One of the hardest hit targets of this war is the home. Home should be a safe place. It should be a place where we experience love, acceptance, and a real sense of who we are as a human being created in the image of God. Home was created to be the environment where God's originals are free to function as He created us to, as we see in Psalms 139:13-14. Often in our fallen world, homes are not a safe or secure place. They become a place of unparalleled destruction from day one where the sins of the fathers are often passed down to the children. It's a cycle of devastation that was never meant to be in the first place!

Our family has been on the radar of investigation for years. We had one son who lived overseas as a missionary and one son who was stateside, working for a company that does a lot of military projects. The connection is evident, but may I tell you that your family is on the radar too? Your family is on the enemy's radar as well. His design and desire is to steal, kill, and destroy. The plan is to divide and conquer at all costs and by all means available to him. He will aim at pitting one family member against another. I call it "no man's land" where everything is fair game. It's a battleground where the barb wired fence would tear to shreds any who try to cross its razor-sharp barbs. His goal is to get us to fight one another and keep us blind to the real enemy. It leaves us all beat up and bloodied by internal battles.

Home becomes a major battlefield where collateral damage piles up! Home is the closest to the heart; therefore, it becomes the bull's eye that the destroyer uses his greatest aggression against. Often home is where children see no reason to listen or honor parents without a real role model. Children get a double message where they are called to do one thing and another thing is lived out before their very eyes. This attitude sets up resentment and internal anger when, "don't do what I do, do what I say to do," flies in the face of their reality. It's a place where fathers or mothers can frustrate the life out of the children by expecting too much or too little, crippling the child for life. I have worked with doctors, lawyers, nurses, and even drug addicts who are either trying to cope with or cut loose from the events of childhood. Childhood memories can pull a sneak attack at the most inconvenient times. Often as children grow up they tend to keep looking in the rearview mirror called reflection, remembering where they "did not measure up." Memory retrieval comes front and center with only a thump of the thought, bringing back rejection from an absent parent, wondering what they did wrong. Children are great absorbers but terrible interpreters. Their reality may be one of emotional abandonment or even abuse. It does not matter whether they are rebels with a cause or a people pleaser trying to make someone happy. It ultimately ends at the same doorstep of control. That is the short and long of it and the heart of the matter.

Control has gotten a bad rap in our generation. It is often an ugly word that is projected as a restriction of our desires and our creativity. Control that insinuates God (or anyone that has authority over us) is holding out on us or wants to rain on our parade. We fear the kind of control that brings the flesh flying right out of us screaming, "Don't tell me what to do!" The Spirit of God, through Paul, warned us this would happen - our fear and false assumptions getting the best of us. Sometimes we are like our children and do not listen attentively. In 2 Timothy 3:1-5, there is a crystal-clear description that might be helpful if posted on every family's door, like the label of side effects on a medicine bottle. Paul uses descriptive words like, "Mark this: There will be savage times in the last days." Whatever kingdom calendar we use, just take note we are now in these days in this generation.

The present reality is enough to give us pause. Paul pushes our reality to an even deeper level when he alerts us to the mystery of inequity, active and aggressive in our day. He pulls out the headline news of our generation as he continues in verse 2, "People will be lovers of themselves, lovers of money, boastful, proud, abusive, disobedient to parents, ungrateful, unholy, without love, unforgiving, slanderous, and without self-control." There is our current world in a mouth full! The number of school shootings alone grabs our attention and leaves us screaming for answers. The day is here when our schools have become war zones. A clear indication of the state of the country spiritually!

The control factor is worth being set free from if it has become a strangle hold. It is worth your attention if it's bent is on making you behave on the outside when on the inside you are standing up shouting, "Never!" It sounds like the law! The law isn't bad; it just shows us how far we have fallen short. The law reveals there is no way on our own to keep it. There's only One who could. If you are a believer, He lives inside of you to fulfill the law within you. A new life inside that inscribes His law on your heart changing your want to, to want to! He alone can give you the desire and power to do what you, at times, really do not want to do as we read in Romans 7. As humans we need to have a constitutional law to maintain justice and order.

Control is worth being set free from when control trips our feet and causes us to fall on the way to the ball. Pleasing others (being people-pleasers) to feel good about ourselves is a form of control. You know the Cinderella story where she wins the prince against all odds? Call her naïve, but the story has a happy ending, right? Beware of a life of glamour and glitz that sells you short of the life of freedom, creativity, and liberty that Christ died and rose again to give you. Everything that shines like gold is not always gold, as an old adage says; that still rings true.

People ask all the time, why do I do what I do? I asked the same question at one time. I bet you have too. To understand the dynamics of the heart we must go to the heart of the issue. At the heart of control springs at least four powerful shoots that explain the dynamics that hold us. What looks to be reasonable or rational becomes a strangle hold if not understood as the reasons for many shoots of behaviors we see in relationships. I learned these liberating truths many years ago training at Grace Life International, which delivered my bound soul over and over again these many years walking with the Lord.

Primarily, the purpose for our desire to control is to keep God from controlling us or getting too close. Control enables us to keep from being overwhelmed by circumstances. Control helps us protect ourselves from others who are motivated to control us through many methods. When we are in control of others we keep them from controlling us by rejecting us or our feeling "used." Control can keep our emotions suppressed or under control. How many songs have been written expounding on "strategies" to live by, which is another way to name control? Only heaven knows.

God is a God of order and creative control. He offers us a control that sets us free, when we understand our Creator and Savior's grace and redemption. The control that gives Him the freedom to demonstrate in our lives what He can do with what we give back to Him. Control that frees us from self-centered living to a life full of adventure is what we are looking for when we have a death grip on control. Freedom comes through releasing our right to control and giving it to the great Redeemer. It's a release from not only our sins, but from ourselves as well. Freedom that gives the Lord the invitation to show up and show off His amazing power to change us from the inside out! It shows us who we really are in Christ, for here is where we begin to learn our true identity. It's a freedom to know His pleasure as Eric Lytle shared in the film, Chariots of Fire as he proclaimed, "I feel His pleasure when I run." It's a freedom to find fulfillment and great joy knowing and doing His will. Freedom to feel the wind in our face as we venture out in our walk of faith with Him! That is the real breath of fresh air.

Yes, you can be a new creation in Christ and live a divided and defeated life. You can choose to run the show and play the game or run the race your way. There will be highs and lows with some small amount of satisfaction in doing it your way. There may even be some "I won" moments to show and tell, but deep down inside, in the dark and secret places, there will come a knock at the door. The inner voice will ask the question, "Is that all there is to life and finding happiness and   satisfaction?"

There was a man named Solomon who was the wisest, wealthiest, most winsome, best-loved, intelligent and good-looking man. He was the man who said there is a time and a season for everything under Heaven. He spared no expense or companionship to get, gain, and control his happiness. In modern times, Solomon would have gotten the man of the year award, written articles in Fortune 500, and taught wealth management classes at Charles Schwab. He wrote multiple books. He managed to get and gain all his heart could ever desire, yet got up one morning and was so down and depressed! He put his pen to parchment and wrote these wrenching words: "Empty, empty, utterly meaningless, everything is meaningless." (Ecclesiastes 1:2 - 12:14) Trust me, his words would not have made the best seller list that year. Most people around him would have suggested he go see his psychiatrist, a good Counselor, or coach, who of course could have helped him if they gave godly insight to his situation. Many in his castle would have surmised he had flipped his kingly crown, and it was rolling down the hill with no return in sight.

This part of the book leaves us feeling depressed with doom and gloom hanging over our heads. We sit with no hope in sight, but it does not end there. At the end of the book in Chapter 12:1 Solomon is wiser for the wear. He calls his readers to remember something we would be wise not to forget. "Remember your Creator in the days of your youth." He calls us to worship with awe and wonder this One who has created us and knows full well. He calls us to recall what it takes to satisfy our longing heart. He calls us to listen and to learn from the journey of the wisest man to ever live. Then he puts down his pen to send his manuscript off to the publisher.

You see this is where the rubber meets the road, right into our driveways and on into our homes. When we forget to remember and don't remember to forget or forgive, relationships in our homes will always suffer. We need to go by the manuscript written by the Creator for the best results in our family dynamics. We must remember He created the family and we cannot improve on His grand design. The order and design of family structure can be healthy and wholesome if we embrace and live filled with His Spirit. Each role He has given us to maximize the relationships as He intended them. If we don't, dads, moms, and children are often lost in the fray. The fall-out does not stop there, though; it tumbles right out into our neighborhoods, into our schools, onto our streets, into our workplace, and into our places of worship. The fiber and foundation of a nation is built on our God and the family the way He designed. The society and wellbeing of any country rest on the health of the family structure. The aim of the enemy is to mess the links and the order up so that a society will tumble down the hill like Jack and Jill. Mark that one down and trace the history to find the proof in the reality.

It's time! It's time to wake up to the real war and use real weapons provided by the original Designer. You are in a battle for your life, and for the lives of your family. See the battle for what it is and win it! This war is not only winnable but this war has been won at the cross, resurrection, ascension, and the outpouring of the Holy Spirit, but we must know the truth, believe it, and live it out in everyday life!

It is time to realize who the real enemy is and is not. Indeed, we have an enemy – really three in one: the world, the flesh, and the devil. The enemy will move anywhere from hell to right up to the gates of heaven if he could stop you from finding healing, health, and wholeness! You have a personal enemy who wants to lie, tell you there is no hope and no do-overs in this life. What is done is done, so just give it up! He will try to convince you to just keep living in the past and that there is no bright hope for your future. He wants to storm the gates of your mind with a shout or a whisper that the impasse you are at is just that - impassable. He will sneer or hiss that you are stuck and you don't deserve to get free again. The spider web is set and the spider is coming for the prey. He mocks you by saying, "you can't forgive what they did without looking back in bondage." All to which I say, like the kids, "Liar, liar pants on fire!" It will only set you free when you say it and mean it. "You can lead a horse to water but you can't make him drink," like my Daddy used to say. That is where I find freedom when I want it so bad for my client and they are not there yet. Patience and prayer is often my only release.

What does the Creator and Redeemer of our souls have to say on this subject? He often said in the Old Testament, listen to me, hear my words and obey. He sets before us life and death as well as freedom and liberty, but we must choose them. He alone can bring healing to the broken. Jeremiah 29:11 says, "For I know the plans I have for you, declares, the Lord, plans to give you *hope* (italics mine)." He said this to me in my darkest hour and deepest distress! You see I am a do-over. "It's never too late to teach old dogs new tricks, or essentially, a new way of living," my Momma said. She was a wise lady whom I loved dearly.

Dear friend, with all the grace and love I can give to you, you are not the exception to that rule. The Lord waits and longs to set you free. The door to the cage is already open, but the choice to fly free is totally up to you. When the pain or problem gets to where you no longer can live this way, you will be ready. Until then I will pray for you. The biggest idols or obstacles you may have in your life may not be others but you.

I would love to sit across the table with you or talk over the phone with no strings attached. I would be interested to hear your story because we all have one. We could explore your options together as we look at where you are and where you want to go. We could walk through the process of how we move forward from being entangled to being set free. We would look at how the Lord equips you for this battle you face every day. We could talk about how to practically put on each piece of armor He has provided by prayer. We would discover how crucial His Word and His Spirit are in winning the war, whether within or without. We would see how there can be no chance to win or change except from the inside out by the renewing of the mind. I repeat it for clarity and emphasis: The Word of God is the only way to live out the freedom you have in Christ and learn who you really. That is biblical cognitive therapy at its finest!

I would like to share some words of wisdom learned on the job. I call it *Life Education 101*. Words alive with power from the Word are found in the fighting fields. I have learned this the hard way, and I do not recommend it! I would challenge you to know four truths that will change your whole life and save your neck like, as it has so often has mine. They are four truths that set us free and keep us free. I will give you my short list to learn intimately. These truths are my life's story and an anchor that is the basis for therapy sessions that I teach and share with others. These will ring true all the days of my life and will be the legacy I leave behind for my family and many others to follow because they are right out of the Book.

The four truths are: Know your God, know yourself, know your enemy, and know your weapons. In that precise order! I wish I would have known and applied these truths many years ago. Here is how it breaks down and fits into your everyday life. Know your God is always first and foremost. He has joined us to Him, and His greatest desire and goal is for us to intimately know Him. It has never meant to be about rules and regulations. These will be included in your walk, but the objective is to know Him deeply. He is the one who loves you and seeks your highest good - period! He is all about relationship. The more you know Him, the more you will love Him, even when you don't understand some of the dark difficult paths you will find yourself on at times. He never leaves you alone - never! I am choosing my words wisely and on purpose. He is in you and He walks with you, all the way, every day in every relationship and situation.

Know yourself, from birth to rebirth you are unique and one of a kind. Psalms 139 shouts that out especially in verse 14. This is not to send you on an ego driven rabbit trail; it is to give you God's perspective of His love and watchful care over you. This has a paradoxical effect on our souls, one of humbling and exalting but always freeing. Knowing the messages, you have heard from birth to rebirth help you understand whether you struggle for acceptance, love, a sense of significance, or self-worth. It will help you identify who in your life has helped form a healthy self-concept and who helped you run into the ditch. This prepackaged programming set you up with feelings and a belief system about yourself, God, and others. Whether you saw how the puzzle pieces fit together, or were able to connect the dots, it is invaluable to make the connection. Either way, it will be important to enable you to get out of the rut of old beliefs and stay out of the pit of self-destruction that you have a bend towards. The object is to get free, not to put blame, shame, or hate on anyone. That is bondage in and of its own. Know who you are now in Christ! You are not the old made over; you are a brand-new creation in Christ (2 Corinthians 5:17). Paul lays out a concept that we can latch onto easily when he commands us to put off the old self (self from birth to rebirth) and to put on the new self (new self from salvation-rebirth to the present), recreated in Christ Jesus. That only happens in the biblical process of the "renewing of the mind" put off then put on (Colossians 3 and Ephesians 4 and 5). This is the real new and your true identity here on earth. It is critical to know these freeing truths, but they are the truths the enemy will fight the hardest to keep you "ignorant of." He does not care how much theological training or degrees you have as long as you, believe, and live out who you are in Christ. The heart of the gospel is Christ in you and the hope of glory. The very life of Christ is in you, and He will live through you when you see the treasure you have in your clay jar.

Know your enemy who hates God and as God's child, he will vent his evil and   destruction at you. Live like you have a personal enemy and you are his target. This is for real, my brothers and sisters! Again, I say this not to cause fear but to give vital enemy information you must have to win the battle. Our perspective should not be of a demon behind every bush. The Sovereign Lord rules, and He means for you to know the real battle and the real enemy by being prepared and in the full armor He has so graciously and lovingly provided for you. Know how the enemy will craft and methodically incorporate his lies into the world system or the culture we live, affecting everyday life, educational system, social media, and even the wide world of sports. The enemy's M. O. is to get us to seek the world's approval, made up of personalities and

philosophies. His goal is to get believers to love it and live for it, while becoming ashamed of the Christ that redeemed us. He does this in subtle and not so subtle ways (1 John 2: 14-17). According to Romans 12:1-2, there is a squeezing going on, and I'm not referring to Charmin's (toilet tissue), which is so squeezable soft. He goes for the inside job as he presents the "deal of your life scheme," tailor made with you in mind, of course. This is a call to arms!

The fourth and final truth I leave with you is to know your weapons: Truth, Righteousness, Peace, Salvation, Shield, and Sword means literally putting on the Lord Jesus Christ. It is a call to offensive (not defensive) living. It is rightly called the armor of God. Daily, we must put on each piece with prayer, realizing exactly what each piece really contains. This is offensive living where we choose to be proactive in our posture and not reactive in our defense. Only the Lord can be our Defender and our Deliver! No human hands can – no matter how hard they try or how much we want them to help – save us.

In closing, let's take a quick look up close and personal at the armor we are to put on and wear. Walk in truth. The Word is always our plumb line. Live in the truth because "He is the way, the truth, and the life (John 14:6)." If it does not pass the truth test, don't tell it and don't believe it! His righteousness becomes ours through His death, burial, resurrection, and indwelling as explained in Romans 5: 17-1. We are righteous, in right relationship and standing, only because of Christ. We have peace because the hostility has ended between us. The war is over and we are invited into a living relationship with Him (Romans 5: 1). Our gift each day is a "peace that passes all understanding," as we surrender everything into His care (Philippians 4: 17). We can choose to panic or to pray, be anxious or to rest the   government on his shoulders (Isaiah 9: 6). I have done both but have so many   more victories these days than defeat, praise you Lord. The helmet of salvation not only secures our relationship, but our salvation, which can save our sanity as we guard our heart and mind. It saves our sanity and sets our mind free by renewing our thoughts each day through the Word of God. Our mind is the control center. Control the mind, control the (wo)man! God changes us from the inside out. We take up the shield of faith or personal trust in the full and finished work of Christ on our behalf. This shield of trust in the goodness, love, and faithfulness of God will put out the flaming arrows the devil hurls our way to try to take us down in fear or doubt. The Spirit of God will hand us His sword, the Word of God for us to defeat the enemy as we speak and live the truth out on the fighting fields of life.

I want to leave you in the presence of so "great a cloud of witnesses," who are   watching the war and cheering us on (Hebrews 12: 1-2). I love the ministry the Lord has called me to in this season of my life. As a Christian Certified Professional Life Coach, I have the awesome privilege to walk some very precious people out of pain and into freedom. Every story is different, but there is only one Savior. It is not me or any other professionally trained person, as good and needful as is this profession. My job is to walk with them through the broken pieces to Jesus. He can and will take the broken pieces and make something beautiful in His time. Others have walked with me to healing and wholeness, and I will be forever grateful for each one of them.

I am blessed to have a few modern-day warriors that have been shining examples to me by wearing their armor so well. Some of these are our new generation leaders who God is raising up and thrusting out into the battle. Nichole Crook Broome, a young lady I was privileged to raise in my home daycare, is one. She is a warrior worshipper with a voice like an angel. She is a Worship Leader and vocalist in her church and has made several CD's. I have watched her wade through the battles that often take place, even in Christian ministries. She is an awesome wife and mom who lives out what she sings. She is the real deal and such an encourager to so many lives.

To my young friend, Trevor King who not only wears his armor, but he literally created a life-sized armor with his own hands. We used his armor in the book. He is an awesome artist and IT (information technology) guy with a passionate heart for missions. What an inspiration he is to this generation.

Thanks to my young friend, Graham Sexton, who is the older brother of the year, year after year. He puts his armor on each day with his servant's heart, helping his parents take loving care of his brother, Will, who has Down's Syndrome. Some days, the battles are heavy but he hangs in there one day at a time. To his mom, Sonya I owe a debt of love. She is a worship warrior if there ever was one. We have walked together through the Word and prayer one battle at a time.

To my dear friend, Becky Seamon, I have watched a pastor's wife, Women's Ministry Leader and awesome writer put each piece of armor on with prayer. She has walked with me through many personal battles, challenging me to stand fast and firm in Christ.

To my fellow missionary mom, Peggy Kean, I give my heartfelt thanks. We have battled often for our children as missionaries overseas. Our hearts have been knit together on so many levels as we have laughed and said, "The Lord saves the best to the last."

My final thanks and respect go to two pastors. First, Pastor David Gales, you taught me all I know of who I am in Christ. I caught what I saw lived out before me, not just preached to me. I have often told him God used him to save my sanity through the Word of God.

To my present pastor, Dr. Terry Faulkenbury, I want to say thank you. You teach the Word of God in power year after year. Your life and lips match which speaks volumes to me (and so many others)!

Both pastors know who they are in Christ and put on their armor each day in prayer. Thank you both for leading us into missions across the street and over the seas. My own children have been blessed and supported like so many other missionaries through your ministries. To our former pastor over missions, Pastor Terry Seamon, thank you for living out missions in every way in your life and ministry. As the Lord has called you and Becky out into missions with Walk Thru the Bible, may your tribe increase.

It's time and you are ready. Ready to rise to the call freer than you were before. You are ready to put on your armor and ready to battle the right enemy. You are   ready to embrace and apply the truths you have learned. You are ready to celebrate who you are in Christ and know why it is so important. It's time to put on your armor in prayer and fight for your life and the lives of your family as well as others.

As you rest in who you are in Christ and His amazing immeasurable love you will have the motivation and passion to win like the victor you are in Christ. It's time! Get ready, get set, run my friend, run, you too will feel His pleasure. Swords drawn right up to the gate!

CHAPTER 7

IT'S TIME TO KNOW THERE IS ANOTHER 9/11 COMING

We have come to the end of our journey together. It has been my joy to walk with you on your unique path. As our paths part, I feel compelled and challenged by the Spirit of God to leave you with a wakeup call. The world is whirling and so are some of our own private lives in this season. We see worldwide chaos escalating at a warp speed never before seen in history.

Geopolitically, those who study prophecy from a Biblical perspective are all standing up and calling for the church to rise up in these last days. We are witnessing a powerful movement of God's Spirit in the last hours. People all over the world are coming to faith in Jesus Christ in amazing ways.

As believers we are being shaken; anxiety and fear are rising. The Spirit of God is challenging us that it is time to know what we don't, to decide which world to love, to cash in, to stop identity theft, and to realize some things don't fit. We have clearly seen in our studies that we are in a fight for our lives. We are not called to be afraid but to be aware and prepared. That is why it is absolutely critical we know who we are in Christ, how to walk in freedom, and how to put on the armor of God daily. We were called for "such a time as this." (Esther 4:14) We are in the generation the Lord has called to serve. We can and must rise up and win in Jesus' name.

We are being told to watch the skies and the winds blowing from the northern front of Russia. Without warning we will see things happen as the world addresses other world powers, giving freedom for undercover aggression in unchallenged power moves. Once again, the world will experience another 9/11. This time, it will be global. If you are reading this book and do not have the assurance that you know Jesus Christ as your Savior, it is time to call upon His name. It's time to realize you are lost, as this book has explained, without any hope in yourself or in anything else to save you from your sins. It is time to repent, turn from your sin and turn to the Savior Who has been calling you. Put your trust alone in His full and finished work on the cross and in the resurrection. He will be born in you today. If you have already asked Him into your heart, please let someone know who can help get you into a healthy congregation of believers so you can grow.

The next great movement for the Church of Jesus Christ is the Rapture. This event will also be without warning. The signs are all in place. This is not meant to be a political statement but a warning of things to come. You

are prepared if you have responded to the truth the Lord has opened to you. The Word calls us to stand and to withstand. I am with you in the battle and in the expectation of the things to come. Carpe Diem!

End Notes

Introduction

1. MandisaVevo, *"He Is With You,"* (June 2, 2009), http://goo.gl/WE8kon.

Chapter One

1. Strong, James, Strong's Exhaustive Concordance of The Bible, The Old Time Gospel Hour Edition, 77.

2. Francis Foulkes, R. V. G. Tasker ed. *Tyndale New Testament Commentaries, The Epistle Of Paul To The Ephesians*, (Grand Rapids, MI: Wm. B. Eerdmans Publishing Company), 1963, 44.

3. John F. Walvood and Roy B. Zuck, eds., *The Bible Knowledge Commentary,*
New Testament Ed. (Victor Books), 1983, 618.

Chapter Two

1. John F. Walvood and Roy B. Zuck, eds., *The Bible Knowledge Commentary,* New Testament Ed. (Victor Books), 1983, 624.

Chapter Five

1. MandisaVevo, *"That's What Scars Are For,"* (August 29, 2013), http://goo.gl/WE8kon.